D1294142

Pretense Design

Design Thinking, Design Theory
Ken Friedman and Erik Stolterman, editors

Per Mollerup

Pretense Design
Surface over Substance

The MIT Press
Cambridge, Massachusetts
London, England

dreyersfond

© 2019 Massachusetts Institute of Technology

All rights reserved. No part of this book may be reproduced in any form by any electronic or mechanical means (including photocopying, recording, or information storage and retrieval) without permission in writing from the publisher.

This book was designed and set in Linotype Univers by Per Mollerup.

Printed and bound in the United States of America.

Library of Congress Cataloging-in-Publication Data is available.

ISBN: 978-0-262-03948-2

10 9 8 7 6 5 4 3 2 1

If things were always what they seemed,
How impoverished would be the imagination of man!
—Pursewarden in Lawrence Durrell, *Balthazar* (1958),
second part of *The Alexandria Quartet*

Contents

Series foreword

As professions go, design is relatively young. The practice of design predates professions. In fact, the practice of design—making things to serve a useful goal, making tools—predates the human race. Making tools is one of the attributes that made us human in the first place.

Design, in the most generic sense of the word, began over 2.5 million years ago when *Homo habilis* manufactured the first tools. Human beings were designing well before we began to walk upright. Four hundred thousand years ago, we began to manufacture spears. By forty thousand years ago, we had moved up to specialized tools.

Urban design and architecture came along ten thousand years ago in Mesopotamia. Interior architecture and furniture design probably emerged with them. It was another five thousand years before graphic design and typography got their start in Sumeria with the development of cuneiform. After that, things picked up speed.

All goods and services are designed. The urge to design—to consider a situation, imagine a better situation, and act to create that improved situation— goes back to our prehuman ancestors. Making tools helped us to become what we are—design helped to make us human.

Today, the word "design" means many things. The common factor linking them is service, and designers are engaged in a service profession in which the results of their work meet human needs.

Design is first of all a process. The word "design" entered the English language in the 1500s as a verb, with the first written citation of the verb dated to the year 1548. *Merriam-Webster's Collegiate Dictionary* defines the verb "design" as "to conceive and plan out in the mind; to have as a specific purpose; to devise for a specific function or end." Related to these is the act of drawing, with an emphasis on the nature of the drawing as a plan or map, as well as "to draw plans for; to create, fashion, execute or construct according to plan."

Half a century later, the word began to be used as a noun, with the first cited use of the noun "design" occurring in 1588. *Merriam-Webster* defines the noun as "a particular purpose held in view by an individual or group; deliberate, purposive planning; a mental project or scheme in which means to an end are laid down." Here, too, purpose and planning toward desired outcomes are central. Among these are "a preliminary sketch or outline showing the main features of something to be executed; an underlying scheme that governs functioning, developing or unfolding; a plan or protocol for carrying out or accomplishing something; the arrangement of elements or details in a product or work of art." Today, we design large, complex process, systems, and services, and we design organizations and structures to produce them. Design has changed considerably since our remote ancestors made the first stone tools.

At a highly abstract level, Herbert Simon's definition covers nearly all imaginable instances of design. To design, Simon writes, is to "[devise] courses of action aimed at changing existing situations into preferred ones" (*The Sciences of the Artificial*, 2nd ed., MIT Press, 1982, p. 129). Design, properly defined, is the entire process across the full range of domains required for any given outcome.

But the design process is always more than a general, abstract way of working. Design takes concrete form in the work of the service professions that meet human needs, a broad range of making and planning disciplines. These include industrial design, graphic design, textile design, furniture design, information design, process design, product design, interaction design, transportation design, educational design, systems design, urban design, design leadership, and design management, as well as architecture, engineering, information technology, and computer science.

These fields focus on different subjects and objects. They have distinct traditions, methods, and vocabularies, used and put into practice by distinct and often dissimilar professional groups. Although the traditions dividing these groups are distinct, common boundaries sometimes form a border. Where this happens, they serve as meeting points where common concerns build bridges. Today, ten challenges uniting the design professions form such a set of common concerns.

Three performance challenges, four substantive challenges, and three contextual challenges bind the design disciplines and professions together as a common field. The performance challenges arise because all design professions:

1. act on the physical world;
2. address human needs; and
3. generate the built environment.

In the past, these common attributes were not sufficient to transcend the boundaries of tradition. Today, objective changes in the larger world give rise to four substantive challenges that are driving convergence in design practice and research. These substantive challenges are:

1. increasingly ambiguous boundaries between artifacts, structure, and process;
2. increasingly large-scale social, economic, and industrial frames;
3. an increasingly complex environment of needs, requirements, and constraints; and
4. information content that often exceeds the value of physical substance.

These challenges require new frameworks of theory and research to address contemporary problem areas while solving specific cases and problems. In professional design practice, we often find that solving design problems requires interdisciplinary teams with a transdisciplinary focus. Fifty years ago, a sole practitioner and an assistant or two might have solved most design problems; today, we need groups of people with skills across several disciplines, and the additional skills that enable professionals to work with, listen to, and learn from each other as they solve problems.

Three contextual challenges define the nature of many design problems today. While many design problems function at a simpler level, these issues affect many of the major design problems that challenge us, and these challenges also affect simple design problems linked to complex social, mechanical, or technical systems. These issues are:

1. a complex environment in which many projects or products cross the boundaries of several organizations, stakeholder, producer, and user groups;
2. projects or products that must meet the expectations of many organizations, stakeholders, producers, and users; and
3. demands at every level of production, distribution, reception, and control.

These ten challenges require a qualitatively different approach to professional design practice than was the case in earlier times. Past environments were simpler. They made simpler demands. Individual experience and personal development were sufficient for depth and substance in professional practice. While experience and development are still necessary, they are no longer sufficient. Most of today's design challenges require analytic and synthetic planning skills that cannot be developed through practice alone.

Professional design practice today involves advanced knowledge. This knowledge is not solely a higher level of professional practice. It is also a qualitatively different form of professional practice that emerges in response to the demands of the information society and the knowledge economy to which it gives rise.

In a recent essay ("Why Design Education Must Change," *Core77*, November 26, 2010), Donald Norman challenges the premises and practices of the design profession. In the past, designers operated on the belief that talent and a willingness to jump into problems with both feet gives them an edge in solving problems. Norman writes:

"In the early days of industrial design, the work was primarily focused upon physical products. Today, however, designers work on organizational structure and social problems, on interaction, service, and experience design. Many problems involve complex social and political issues. As a result, designers have become applied behavioral scientists, but they are woefully undereducated for the task. Designers often fail to understand the complexity of the issues and the depth of knowledge already known. They claim that fresh eyes can produce novel solutions, but then they wonder why these solutions are seldom implemented, or if implemented, why they fail. Fresh eyes can indeed produce insightful results, but the eyes must also be educated and knowledgeable. Designers often lack the requisite understanding. Design schools do not train students about these complex issues, about the interlocking complexities of human and social behavior, about the behavioral sciences, technology, and business. There is little or no training in science, the scientific method, and experimental design."

This is not industrial design in the sense of designing products, but industry-related design, design as thought and action for solving problems and imagining new futures. This new MIT Press series of books emphasizes strategic design to create value through innovative products and services, and it emphasizes design as service through rigorous creativity, critical inquiry, and an ethics of respectful design. This rests on a sense of understanding, empathy, and appreciation for people, for nature, and for the world we shape through design. Our goal as editors is to develop a series of vital conversations that help designers and researchers to serve business, industry, and the public sector for positive social and economic outcomes.

We will present books that bring a new sense of inquiry to the design, helping to shape a more reflective and stable design discipline able to support a stronger profession grounded in empirical research, generative concepts, and the solid theory that gives rise to what W. Edwards Deming described as profound knowledge (*The New Economics for Industry, Government, Education*, MIT Center for Advanced Engineering Study, 1993). For Deming, a physicist, engineer, and designer, profound knowledge comprised systems thinking and the understanding of processes embedded in systems; an understanding of variation and the tools we need to understand variation; a theory of knowledge; and a foundation in human psychology. This is the beginning of "deep design"—the union of deep practice with robust intellectual inquiry.

A series on design thinking and theory faces the same challenges that we face as a profession. On one level, design is a general human process that we use to understand and to shape our world. Nevertheless, we cannot address this process or the world in its general, abstract form. Rather, we meet the challenges of design in specific challenges, addressing problems or ideas in a situated context. The challenges we face as designers today are as diverse as the problems clients bring us. We are involved in design for economic anchors, economic continuity, and economic growth. We design for urban needs anrural needs, for social development and creative communities. We are involved with environmental sustainability and economic policy, agriculture, competitive crafts for export, competitive products and brands for micro-enterprises, developing new products for bottom-of-pyramid markets, and redeveloping old products for mature or wealthy markets. Within the framework of design, we are also challenged to design for extreme situations, for biotech, nanotech, and new materials, and to design for social business, and we face conceptual challenges for worlds that do not yet exist, such as the world beyond the Kurzweil singularity—and for new visions of the world that does exist.

The Design Thinking, Design Theory series from the MIT Press will explore these issues and more—meeting them, examining them, and helping designers to address them.

Join us in this journey.

Ken Friedman   Erik Stolterman
Editors, Design Thinking, Design Theory Series

Appearance first

Pretense Design discusses a design[1] category that, in spite of its omnipresence, until now has flown under the radar of researchers and authors. Pretense design pretends to be something it is not, hence the term. All thinking builds on concepts; design thinking[2] needs the concept of pretense design. We think much more clearly about the pretense design category when it has a name.

Pretense design includes all kinds of physical artifacts: designed objects such as materials, products, buildings, and built environments which send persuasive messages that to some degree deviate from the object's substance. The Italian word *dietrologia*—literally "behindology"—meaning that there is something different behind the surface, exactly describes the defining quality.

The designers and users of pretense design find it advantageous to project an image more or less different from the substance of the designed object, something they consider preferable to the default appearance. Traditional design thinking does not consider this situation.

Honesty is a time-honored principle in professional design. It is a basic ingredient in conventional design wisdom reflected in catchphrases such as "Form follows function" and "Truth to materials." Writers on design tell us, professional designers confirm, and teachers repeat, that good design is honest design; good design shows its true identity. The outsides of designed objects should be honest representations of their insides as well as the intentions behind. What we see should herald what we get.

[1] We shall use the word "design" exclusively to refer to physical artifacts—in contrast to events, plans, laws, etc. Also, we shall use the word "design" to refer to both the process and the result of the process.

[2] In *Pretense Design*, "design thinking" means "thinking about design"—not thinking about an idealized way in which designers think or ought to think.

However, not all designed materials, products, buildings, and environments meet this honesty ideal pedantically. The appearance of artifacts may enhance, embellish, obscure, hide, or contradict their substance. Designed materials, products, buildings, and environments with an intended discrepancy between surface and substance, between appearance and reality, make up their own genre: pretense design. The outside expresses the inside in a deviating, persuasive way. These objects pretend in order to persuade.

Although firmly embedded in physical design, pretense design is, as far as pretense is concerned, a communication issue and should be addressed as such. Pretense design is design rhetoric: it delivers persuasive arguments. The surface deliberately misrepresents the substance in order to change the attitudes of the audience.

Even though it hasn't had a name until now, pretense design is ubiquitous. Cosmetics, clothes, furniture, food, cars, buildings, gardens, whole cities, and landscapes may be, or contain elements of, pretense design. Pretense design is most often attractive, amusing, or convenient, but it can also be fraudulent. The outcome depends on intention, execution, and application.

Pretense Design touches a plethora of diverse subjects, not pursuing every one in great detail. The focus has been on describing a new design category: What is it? Why is it? Where is it?

Per Mollerup
Copenhagen, 2018

Pretense design: Design where an object's appearance differs from the object's true nature in a persuasive way.

1

**Figure 1
Landscape garden,
Castle Ashby,
Northamptonshire,
United Kingdom**
Showing and hiding
are the means of
pretense design. This
landscape garden
hides something.
See p. 98.

Object language

For the great majority of mankind are satisfied with appearances, as though they were realities, and are often more influenced by the things that seem than by those that are.
—Niccolò Machiavelli (1469–1527)

It is only shallow people who do not judge by appearances.
—Oscar Wilde (1854–1900)

Object language
Objects talk

Designed objects are tools; they have practical functions which are their *raison d'être*. If designed objects had no practical function, we would not need them and they would probably not exist. Designed objects have a form, which according to conventional design thinking is determined by the function. The form that follows function as a rule reveals the intended function. But that is not all.

In *The Stones of Venice*, John Ruskin suggested that the duty of buildings is to shelter and to talk (1880, 36). The buildings' practical duty is to provide protection from weather and violence, while their talking duty deals with recording facts and expressing feelings. Buildings may tell us what they are, how they were made, by whom they were made, for whom they were made, when they were made, what they are made of, what they can be used for, how they should be used, and more.

Along with this indicative information, buildings may symbolically point to cultural values considered important to designers, users, and spectators. Some of this symbolic information may be apparent to everyone, while some of it may be confined to architecturally literate onlookers who know the code.

Buildings are not alone. The principle of inanimate things talking applies to all kinds of physical artifacts. Materials, products, and environments talk; they carry more or less easily understandable visual messages.

Figure 2
30 St Mary Axe, London
Design: Norman Foster & Ken Shuttleworth, 2004
This landmark edifice in London's primary financial district is popularly known as "The Gherkin." More important than the vegetable similarity is the building's message of modernity.

2

Object language
Objects talk

Grant McCracken (1990) warns against
stretching the object language metaphor too far.
Real language, spoken or written, has a cluster of
properties absent in the message-carrying potential
of physical objects. Even then, physical objects
may be quite eloquent and quite enduring in their
messages.

The appearance of physical artifacts can be
more or less symbolically interesting and aesthetically
pleasing. Fashion is a case in point, but symbolism
and aesthetics are also in play in more mundane
objects. For some buildings and products, their
appearance counts as much as, or more than, their
technical function. The appearance impresses and
persuades; it serves a rhetorical purpose. Pretense
design is material rhetoric.

Pretense design reflects a movement of
the users' interest from technical functionality
to communication, from substance to surface.
Communication takes command, to paraphrase
Sigfried Giedion's seminal book *Mechanization Takes
Command* (1948). The outside dominates the inside.
What you see is an essential part of what you get.
As part of this development, designers assign added
weight to the communicative sides of designed
objects. This is reflected in the interest in product
semantics and design rhetoric, soon to be discussed.

In *Pretense Design*, the word "talk" is used
metaphorically for "carry messages." There are
always people behind the talking objects, be they
producers or users. The inanimate objects are media
with no intentions of their own.

3

**Figure 3
Bollitore 9091
Design: Richard
Sapper, 1984
Manufacturer:
Alessi, Italy**
Alessi specializes
in products that
transcend their
technical function:
They talk.

Object language
Objects deceive

The message carried by materials, products, buildings, and environments may be more or less honest, and may reflect the substance more or less truthfully. Like spoken language, the language of artifacts may bend the truth by making statements that are less than completely true. Objects can deceive. This idea is not new; often-repeated adages such as "Don't judge a book by its cover" and "All that glitters is not gold" provide circumstantial evidence. Potential users are warned, as the sheer existence of these proverbs hints at the possible existence of misleading surfaces. Most of the time, however, we ignore these warnings. Judging substances by their surfaces is our default way of interacting with the world. When we see what looks like an apple, we take it for an apple. Life would be unbearable if we could not trust our vision—and other senses—most of the time. However, there are howevers.

Pretense design—design with an intentional discrepancy between surface and substance—is by definition not totally authentic. The missing authenticity[1] may concern whatever the object talks about: its provenance, its design, its purpose, its material, its construction, its use, and its user. The object's indicative function is compromised.

Pretense design is not necessarily a bad thing. In fact, it is most often a good thing. We are, if not surrounded, then frequently confronted, by objects that are not exactly what they appear to be, but which exactly because of this lack of congruence make our life richer, more tolerable, more beautiful, more amusing. Our life would be poorer without pretense design.

[1] "The missing authenticity" discussed here should not be mistaken for the often referred to authenticity presented by Walter Benjamin in *The Work of Art in the Age of Mechanical Reproduction* (2010). Benjamin considers authenticity a quality restricted to works of art produced by the artist.

4

Figure 4
Teatro Olimpico,
Vicenza, Italy
Design: Andrea
Palladio, 1580–1585
Theater is pretense.
Teatro Olimpico is
the world's oldest
existing indoor
theater. Vincenzo
Scamozzi completed
the building after
Palladio's death, and
designed the famous
forced perspective,
the world's oldest
stage set.

Object language
Objects deceive

Pretense design is by definition intentional: somebody deliberately designs a counterfactual surface that misrepresents the substance. The minds behind pretense design see their advantage in bending the truth. The reason may be a quest for beauty, or amusement, or a desire to substitute something which for one reason or another is not available or recommended. Finally, pretense design may—of course—be created and used for unethical, even outright criminal, deception.

We shall discuss the motives, the means, the perceptibility, the communication elements, and the roles of pretense design in some detail before presenting a suite of pretense design instances in fields extending from computer fonts to warships, from hair dyeing to whole cities.

Object language
Bending the truth

False, the antonym of "true," is more than a binary position. False resides in a continuum spanning from the white lie to the most deceitful untruth. The three following examples illustrate the range.

Mortimer is a young man who is interviewed for a new job. He is determined not to hide his light under a bushel. He spins, emphasizes his good sides, and omits less attractive qualities, but he does not invent false academic merits or fictive job positions. He is not a liar. On the other hand, nobody expects job applicants to advertise their vulnerabilities. Mortimer gives the truth a beauty check: he romanticizes, presents the truth in an edited format. Our self-presentation in everyday life is always edited in some way or another (Goffman 1959).

"To ride, to shoot with a bow, to speak the truth" was a Herodotus-inspired slogan fancied by Karen Blixen—alias Isak Dinesen, Osceola, and Pierre Andrézel[1]—author of *Babette's Feast* and *Out of Africa*. Her brother, author and adventurer Thomas Dinesen, had his reservations: "Well, in fact, my sister couldn't ride or shoot an arrow, and she never told the truth" (both quoted from Thurman 1982, 165). Writers of fiction have a professional license to fabricate. Novels, plays, and films are acknowledged refuges for fantasy. Readers and spectators expect fiction. The truth is on standby.

The restaurant menu advertises "the season's vegetables." The guest takes for granted that "season" means "current season," but the chef uses canned vegetables. That is fraud; the truth is suspended.

[1] Pseudonyms, noms de plume, are an acknowledged way of hiding true authorship.

Object language
Bending the truth

The truth edited, the truth on standby, and the truth suspended are three positions along the truth-bending continuum that without sharp distinctions goes from the slightly embellished truth to the outright lie. These three examples deal with speech and writing. But spoken and written language are not alone in dealing flexibly with truth. Materials, products, buildings, and entire environments can also carry messages that more or less innocently doctor reality.

Pretense design covers a truth-bending continuum of options from the most innocent embellishment of reality to criminal deception. The dress that makes the buxom girl appear slender populates the same truth-bending continuum as the "borrowed" military uniform that in 1906 enabled the proverbial Prussian Captain of Köpenick to confiscate more than 4,000 marks from the municipal treasury.[1]

Being much more than a dichotomous position, material truth-bending resembles traditional lies. They are not just lies; they are situated on a continuum from more to less severe. In his essay on lying, *De mendacio* (395 CE), Saint Augustine suggested that lies serving a good purpose belong to the latter group (Augustine 2017). In her analysis of contemporary lying, Bella DePaolo (2010) distinguishes between white and not-so-white lies, as well as between self-centered lies and other-oriented lies. Self-centered lies are told for psychological reasons, to support or protect the liar, but can also be told for personal gain. Other-oriented lies are told to support or protect others than the liar. To tell an ill person that she looks well is an other-oriented white lie, more humane than pedantically true.

Three positions on the truth-bending continuum:
- The truth edited
- The truth on standby
- The truth suspended

[1] The Captain of Köpenick, as Friedrich Wilhelm Voigt became known, was sentenced to four years in prison, but was pardoned after two years by Kaiser Wilhelm II, and became a folk hero as *Der Hauptmann von Köpenick* ("Wilhelm Voigt," En.wikipedia.org 2017).

5

The truth-bending involved in pretense design
is basically self-centered. It benefits the pretender.

Figure 5
Masks for Carnival
in Venice, Italy
The truth is on
standby.

Object language
Product semantics

In *Pretense Design*, to "design" means "to give shape to artifacts" and "shape given to artifacts," in which "shape" is understood in its widest sense. All manmade objects are designed, because somebody has determined their shape. It is the designer's job to enable the function of an artifact in the best possible way with the given technological and economic possibilities and constraints.

But manmade objects serve more than purely technical functions. To function technically, physical artifacts must also serve a communication function. To fulfill its technical function, a photocopier must also communicate. It must explain what it is (its identity), what it can be used for (its affordance), and how it should be used (its operation). These messages are especially important in new products and in technically complicated products.

A photocopier or any other appliance can explain its correct use in three different ways. First, the appliance can be self-explanatory; everybody can see how a hammer works; most photocopiers are less expressive. Second, the appliance can have labels with instructional text. Third, the appliance can be accompanied by external user instructions. As users, we prefer self-explanatory products. We prefer a drill that by its sheer form explains how we should mount the drill, how we should hold the tool, how we should switch the machine on and off, and how we can control direction and speed.

6

Figure 6
Riga-Minox
Subminiature
camera with
Minostigmat 3,5
F=15 lens
Design: Walter Zapp,
1936
Manufacturer: VEF,
Latvia
Product semantics
deal with the
indicative information
given by the product's
design: What is it?
What can it be used
for? How should it be
operated?

There is a subtle transition from self-explanatory products to products with instructional labels. A green Start and red Stop button on a drilling machine are part of the self-explanatory product design, while ON and OFF text should be classified as labels. The color of the buttons is an integrated part of the product design. The text is something added.

Separate user instructions are often problematic. They tend to be absent when needed. They are frequently written in a not preferred language. They are sometimes written for several models or for another model than the one at hand, or they are difficult to understand. Modern appliances with electronic screens or displays telling what to do next negotiate most of these tribulations.

Product semantics deal with the ways products explain themselves—in other words, how designers invest and users "read" functional meaning in products. A good door handle shows immediately what it is for and how it should be operated. The more expressive the product semantics, the fewer labels and the less written user instructions are needed.

Pretense design may compromise product semantics. If pretense design obscures the identity and perceivable affordance of an object, it will also compromise its self-explanation. A secret door that can be understood as a door only by those who know a code obscures its operation for those not informed.

Product semantics explain the identity and intended use of designed objects. Jochen Gros (1987) suggested codifying product functions in a way that situates product semantics in the greater human-machine picture.

First, Gros divided product functions into practical functions versus product language functions. While the practical functions concern the physical functioning, the product language functions have to do with the sensual side of the object—that is, whatever can be sensed about it.

Second, Gros divided the product language functions into formal aesthetic functions versus semantic functions. The formal aesthetic functions feed on the product language seen as independent of the meaning of the content: shape, surface, color, etc.—that is, the grammar of the product language. The semantic functions are the linguistic functions that carry meaning.

Third, Gros divided the semantic functions into indicating functions versus symbol functions. The indicating functions describe the object directly, whereas the symbol functions characterize the object with reference to something outside the product, through its similarity with something else.

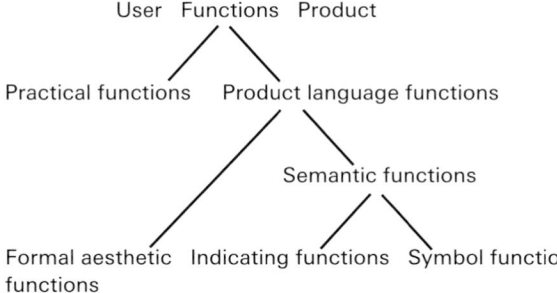

User Functions Product

Practical functions   Product language functions

Semantic functions

Formal aesthetic Indicating functions Symbol functions
functions

Figure 7
The Offenbach model
(Gros 1987, 70)
Our translation. The semantic functions deal with the ways products explain themselves.

While indicating functions address the users'
understanding, design rhetoric addresses both the
users' understanding and feelings, but importantly
also the understanding and feelings of the users'
onlookers. Users of pretense design products use
them as markers when projecting their own (and their
belongings') identity, showing themselves and their
surroundings who (they like to think) they "really" are.

Design rhetoric is a visual outpost of rhetoric,
the discipline that traditionally deals with spoken
and written language. Classical rhetoric as practiced
in ancient Greece is the art of finding and delivering
persuasive arguments. Aristotle suggested that
rhetoric should be used for political, forensic, and
ceremonial purposes. Since then, experts of all
kinds of communication, including designers and
architects, have made claims on rhetoric. Physical
artifacts are the media of design rhetoric.

Aristotle pointed at three rhetorical elements:
logos, ethos, and pathos. Logos is the construction of
logical arguments, and addresses the understanding
of the audience. Ethos is the projection of the
speaker's character, authority, and credibility; it
addresses the confidence of the audience. Finally,
pathos has to do with arguments that address
the feelings of the audience. Each of these three
elements can with some imagination be seen to apply
to design rhetoric. Then, logos refers to the rationality
of the object, explaining why it is as it is to function
well. Ethos hints at the competence of the makers.
Finally, pathos delivers arguments that touch the
feelings of the users.

A gentleman's watch may visually hint at its logical construction. If the lay audience cannot see and understand the hidden mechanics, they can judge *pars pro toto* from the logically designed dial and the well-crafted case. This is the logos. The label, say IWC or Rolex, may point at the maker's credibility and authority. Likewise, a certain recognizable style can create credibility by acting as a company's or designer's signature. This is the ethos. Finally, the watch's unequivocal manliness may please the feelings of a certain segment of users. This is the pathos.

Modern fashion labels such as Armani and Ralph Lauren also sell watches. However, the ethos backing these watches is based on the labels' merits in the clothing trade rather than in horology. Armani and Lauren are known for fashionable apparel rather than durable, technically advanced products. Similarly, timepieces by other opportunistic watch marketers such as MontBlanc and Victorinox probably get limited ethos credit for watch-making. These companies earned their technical credibility and authority in fields far away from advanced watch-making: making excellent fountain pens and robust Swiss Army knives, respectively.

Critics of considering product design as communication may ask questions such as, Who is the sender? What is the message? Who is the receiver? The pretense design answer is obvious. Somebody (the sender) uses the object (the medium with its message) to persuade somebody (the addressee). Pretense design is communication.

All people use rhetoric to persuade, to convince somebody of something. This includes designers in their professional capacity. Designers apply rhetoric to promote their designs in words and—importantly—in deeds equaling design. Richard Buchanan suggested that "design is an art of thought directed to practical action through the persuasiveness of objects" (1985, 7)—in other words, designers do more than make objects; they give persuasive arguments a physical form, later to be read by prospective and actual users and onlookers.

Rhetoric can influence opinions about the past (as in legal rhetoric), the future (as in political rhetoric), and the present (as in ceremonial rhetoric). Buchanan (1985, 20) suggested that the persuasive arguments invested in designed objects partly demonstrate the use of already known scientific principles, and partly suggest the potential of the objects. In the case of pretense design that, for instance, pretends to be older than it really is, design rhetoric obviously attempts to recreate something from the past while suggesting a solution for the present and the future.

Design rhetoric addresses the product language functions, including formal aesthetic functions, indicating functions, and symbol functions, as in Gros's model of design functions (see fig. 7). These can all be part of persuasive arguments. Pretense design has to do with indicative and symbol functions. Both categories can be part of deceptive statements.

Figure 8
Porsche 911 G-series, Carrera coupe, 1988 Manufacturer: Porsche, Germany
Design rhetoric deals with finding and presenting design arguments that impress and persuade prospective buyers, owners, and observers.

Aesthetic functions are not relevant to pretense design since meaning is not part of the aesthetic functions, and pretense design is all about meaning. The color of a sports car is basically an aesthetic function, for example. To the extent that the car's British racing green color suggests "classic English sports car," the color is also a symbol function. If this car is not a classic English sports car, pretense design is at work.

8

Messages mediated by objects can—like spoken and written messages—be true, almost true, or absolutely untrue. They comply with Umberto Eco's definition of semiotics: "the discipline studying everything which can be used in order to lie" (1997, 7). What objects say about identity, provenance, function, operation, user identity, and objectives can be true, false, or anything in between. In *Pretense Design* we shall use the verb "pretend" and the noun "pretense" rather than "lie" to avoid stigmatizing the *bona fide* branch of truth-bending design.

Designed artifacts pretend on behalf of designers, manufacturers, sellers, and users to gain advantages. Pretense is a means to ends. If successful, pretense design makes somebody believe something that the pretender prefers to project rather than the pedantic truth. Showing without being, the modus operandi of pretense design, goes beyond the Shakespearean dichotomy, "to be or not to be." Pretense design is and is not.

Pretense design delivers material short cuts from existing situations to preferred situations, to use Herbert Simon's definition of design.[1] The motivation can be dislike of the present situation, desire for the preferred situation, or both. A wearer of a toupee, a small hairpiece to cover baldness, probably wants to hide his true hirsute status. The Elvis impersonator wants to be The King, and the teen who bleaches her hair probably dislikes her natural mouse shade as much as she desires the attractive blondness.

[1] *Everyone designs who devises courses of action aimed at changing existing situations into preferred ones* —Simon 1996, 111

Humans are not alone in adjusting their appearance to gain advantages. Animals also pretend: they imitate, exaggerate, underplay, and suppress to change not preferred situations into preferred ones. With animals, as with humans, the pretense can be permanent or situation-specific. The walking stick and several other insects pretend permanently to be something that they are not, while chameleons and other species save their disguise for special occasions such as attack, defense, foraging, or courtship. Pretense on demand.

We shall classify pretense design according to four objectives, all aimed at changing existing situations into preferred ones: beautification, amusement, substitution, and deception. This classification aims at giving a better understanding of pretense design. Thinking builds on concepts; concepts build on classification.

• Beautification pretense is the aesthetic adjustment of the default situation. The truth is edited, on standby, or suspended.

• Amusement pretense deals with situational otherness. The truth is on standby or suspended.

• Substitution pretense plays on likeness to the unavailable substituted condition. The truth is on standby or suspended.

• Deception pretense, or cheating, takes place at the expense of the audience. The truth is suspended.

Pretense design objectives:
• Beautification
• Amusement
• Substitution
• Deception

Objective	Key quality	Truth-bending
Beautification	Improvement	Edited / Standby / Suspended
Amusement	Otherness	Standby / Suspended
Substitution	Likeness	Standby / Suspended
Deception	Cheating	Suspended

Pretense design objectives

The four pretense design objectives are not watertight compartments, nor mutually exclusive by any means. A trompe l'oeil painting may, apart from providing amusement, also serve as beautification.

Pretense design is, as already established, a communication issue and has several resemblances with spoken and written language, including such phenomena as euphemism, analogy, synonymy, and lying.

Figure 9
Faux furs
Beautification, amusement, and substitution are not mutually exclusive pretense objectives. They could all be in play in these faux furs flashed at President Obama's inauguration in 2013.

9

Beautification pretense involves a surface adjustment of a human or material thing. The basic sought-after quality is beauty, but symbolism may also be in play. To the extent that a tanned body is not only considered more beautiful than an untanned body but also is read as a sign of good health and success, the beautification also involves a symbolic pretense. No matter what, beautification pretense is about presenting something in a nicer way; to use a linguistic analogy: it is a euphemism.

In contrast to beautification pretense, amusement pretense is first and foremost about symbolic appearance; aesthetic appearance is a side effect. The pretense medium is most often a material thing, but it can also be a human. Amusement pretense may involve simulation of a wide range of qualities considered attractive: time, age, material, function, relentlessness, and more. Not all users of amusement design objects may distinguish between symbolic and aesthetic aspects, but may just consider their Louis Seize reproduction furniture more attractive than contemporary furniture. But some users may enjoy the travel through time, while still others may concentrate on the beauty with no thoughts about the period. The linguistic analogy of amusement pretense design is analogy: something different combined with something shared.

Substitution pretense is about keeping up appearances. The pretense medium is most often material things, but can also include human parts, in the case of prosthetics. If totally successful, the substitute is not distinguishable from what is being replaced. While beautification pretense and amusement pretense involve changes in aesthetic and symbolic appearance, substitution pretense aims to keep appearance unchanged. To use a linguistic analogy, a successful substitution offers material synonyms.

Deception pretense is about cheating in function and/or substance. The pretense medium is humans or material things, and involves aesthetic as well as symbolic appearance; changes happen on both dimensions. The linguistic parallel to deception pretense design is lies—big lies.

Pretense design is an intentionally counterfactual rewriting of a reality considered in need of change. The rewriting is pleasant in the case of beautification and amusement pretense; practical in substitution and deception pretense; benign for addressees in beautification, amusement, and (most often) substitution; and malign for addressees of deception and (sometimes) substitution.

The three truth-bending classes—truth edited, truth on standby, and truth suspended—codify degrees of pretense: how much the message projected differs from the truth. The objectives—beautification, amusement, substitution, and deception—codify the intentions of pretense design. Modes, a third way of classifying pretense design, codify how pretense design deviates from the truth. While the truth-bending classes address quantitative differences between pretense design and the truth, the modes deal with qualitative differences: *how* rather than *how much*.

In his *Essays, Civil and Moral* from 1625, Francis Bacon devised three ways in which a person could purposely hide and veil his self: secrecy, dissimulation, and simulation. To Bacon, secrecy meant keeping a low profile: "when a man leaves himself without observation, or without hold to be taken, what he is." Dissimulation hides something unwanted; it is "when a man lets fall signs and arguments, that he is not that he is." Finally, simulation presents something untrue: "when a man industriously and expressly feigns and pretends to be that he is not" (Bacon 1909–1914).

Pretense design is not limited to hiding and veiling, nor to personal conduct. All four pretense design objectives—beautification, amusement, substitution, and deception—include attention-grabbing activities such as showing off and bluffing, which call for other modes.

We shall classify pretense design in four modes: overstatement, understatement, simulation, and hiding. Overstatement and understatement fall outside Bacon's hide-and-veil categories, whereas simulation parallels Bacon's simulation. Finally, hiding covers Bacon's dissimulation and secrecy.

Pretense design modes:
- Overstatement
- Understatement
- Simulation
- Hiding

Pretense design modes	Francis Bacon's hide-and-veil categories
Overstatement	
Understatement	
Simulation	Simulation
Hiding	Dissimulation
	Simulation

Pretense design modes compared with Francis Bacon's hide-and-veil categories

Overstatement is—without exaggeration—the most often practiced and simplest mode of pretense design. High heels, four-wheel drives with bull bars, and excessively technical domestic espresso machines all overstate qualities considered attractive.

Understatement deals with downplay. Clothes that make the wearer appear slimmer fall into this category.

Overstatement and understatement can obviously be seen as two sides of the same coin, insofar as overstating one quality implies understating the opposite quality.

Simulation includes design of surfaces that deliberately misrepresent the substance. Set pieces, props, and theater costumes constitute the aristocracy of fabrication. Wigs, artificial limbs, and coffee substitutes also belong to this category.

Hiding means disappearing from sight and other senses. Most military camouflage resides in this category. The colloquial metaphor "flying under the radar" alludes to this pretense design mode. Simulation, in some cases, also hides something not wanted from the public. The Guy Fawkes masks (fig. 10) show allegiance to the group Anonymous while hiding the protesters' faces. Rather than being sharply divided and mutually exclusive categories, the four pretense design modes should be seen as possibly concurrent qualities.

The four pretense design modes combined with the four objectives inform the four-by-four matrix with sixteen fields available for pretense design.

Objectives	Modes			
	Overstatement	Understatement	Simulation	Hiding
Beautification	x	x	x	x
Pleasure	x	x	x	x
Substitution	x	x	x	x
Deception	x	x	x	x
Pretense design objectives and modes				

Figure 10
Guy Fawkes masks at Anonymous demonstration, London, 2008
The masks' pretense design mode is hiding.

10

Much pretense design is overt: the misrepresentation takes place in the open. The openness is part of the game. To hide the fashionista's stilettos that make her legs appear longer, her feet smaller, and her walking more intriguing would be counterproductive to the idea of dressing up. Theaters also do their magic in the open. The scene, complete with backdrop, set pieces, and props, pretends to be something that it is not, but the aesthetic distance insures that the audience knows where they are: this is theater, not reality. "Innocent fraudulence," not an oxymoron here, describes the business of this much-loved province of pretense design. Overt pretense design is, as a rule, innocent. Its opposite, covert pretense design, can be innocent or fraudulent.

Covert pretense design takes place when the pretender seriously tries to hide the true character of the designed object. A person with an artificial limb may want to hide his prosthetic as well as possible. A seller of confectionery may try to hide the fact that the packaging contains more air than sweets and chocolate. Covert pretense design is *bona fide* and innocent in the first case, but *mala fide* and fraudulent in the second case.

Umberto Eco coined the term "aberrant decoding" to describe a situation where the receiver of a message understands something not intended by the sender (1972, 132). The sender of covert pretense design—i.e., the designer, manufacturer, seller, or user—wants the receiver to misunderstand something. Understanding the truth behind the pretense would in this case be aberrant decoding, as long as the sender did not intend it. Not seeing the truth would be aberrant decoding as far as the reality is concerned.

Pretense design perceptibility classes:
• Overt
• Covert

11

Figure 11
Vienna Magic,
Vienna, Austria
Overtness is a natural
part of good magic.
The audience know
they are being fooled.

Pretense design involves three roles: producer, pretender, and addressee. These roles may be distributed in different ways. The producer and the pretender may be the same party. That is the case when a company manufactures design copies of famous furniture and sells the copies as originals: the company is both producer and pretender, while the naive customer is the addressee. If the customer, on the other hand, perhaps informed explicitly or by the low price, is well aware of the provenance of the furniture but nevertheless presents it as original to his friends, the roles will change. Now the manufacturer is the producer and only that, while the customer is the pretender, and the customer's friends and other acquaintances become addressees.

Pretenders pretend in order to impress those around them, but sometimes also to impress themselves. Then they are themselves addressees. We don't dress up exclusively to impress other people, for example. As pretenders we can double as addressees, and sometimes as producers as well, just as we can write a letter to ourselves.

Some objects only become pretense design through pretending use. A firefighter's uniform only becomes pretense design when worn at a fancy dress party by someone who is not a firefighter.

Pretense design comprises objects used in social interaction with the purpose of impressing something on somebody. This process involves three communication elements: medium, message, and pretense.

Pretense design roles:
- Producer
- Pretender
- Addressee

Communication elements:
- Medium
- Message
- Pretense

The pretense medium is whatever canvas is used for pretense design: a part of the human body, a product, a material, or something else. The pretense message is a special expression of the pretense medium designed to advocate the pretense, some counterfactual suggestion. The pretense is the addressee's understanding, as intended by the pretender.

Figure 12
Mannequins in shop window, Chanel, Rue Cambon, Paris
Cost-saving pretense design. The truth is edited, the objective is amusement and substitution, the mode is simulation, and the perceptibility level is overt. Chanel doubles as producer and pretender. Passersby are addressees.

12

Objects, like words, may have a figurative meaning
apart from their literal meaning. The literal meaning
is understood, while the figurative meaning is
felt. Linguistics uses the terms "denotation" and
"connotation" to distinguish between these two
kinds of meaning. A rose denotes a red flower with
a green stem and leaves. To some people it also
connotes love. While the denotation is shared by
"all" people, the connotation may be restricted to
some. The quotation marks around "all" restrict
the understanders to those familiar with the type
of pretense medium. A person who has never
heard of or seen mahogany before will not identify
a mahogany cabinet as such. Denotation depends
on the viewer, and so—and even more—does
connotation. Pretense design depends on both
denotation and connotation, which both depend on
the audience.

Most pretense design deals with some kind of
lookalike; it denotes something false. False eyelashes
denote eyelashes (false ones), theater sets denote
certain environments (false ones), a camouflaged
cannon may denote cowshed (false), and so on.
Connotation plays no part in this type of pretense
design.

False denotation /
No connotation

Some pretense design denotes something true
and connotes something false. A landlubber's boat
shoes denote boat shoes (true) and connotes sailor
(false).

True denotation /
False connotation

Some pretense design denotes something
false and connotes something true. A Mac
computer's trash bin icon denotes an analog trash bin
(false) and connotes ejection (true).

False denotation /
True connotation

Finally, some pretense design both denotes something false and connotes something false. A (lay) carnival-goer's fake stethoscope denotes stethoscope (false) and connotes physician (false).

False denotation / False connotation

	True denotation	False denotation
No connotation	True denotation No connotation	False denotation No connotation
True connotation	True denotation True connotation	False denotation True connotation
False connotation	True denotation False connotation	False denotation False connotation

Meaning-building in pretense design

The combinations true denotation / no connotation and true denotation / true connotation involve no deviation from truth and, and therefore exclude pretense design.

In pretense design, denotation and connotation may both refer to owners/users and objects.

Object language
A theory of deception

Pretense design has until now defied description, let alone precise codification. However, J. Bowyer Bell and Barton Whaley (1991) presented a general theory of deception marked by their background in military studies.

Bell and Whaley distinguish between deception meant to hide the truth, which they call "level-one deception," and deception that puts forward a falsehood, a practice they call "level-two deception." Bell and Whaley hold that deception showing the false always hides the truth, while deception hiding the truth doesn't necessarily present a falsehood. In other words: showing the false is a subset of hiding the truth. Bell and Whaley divide each of the two main classes into three subclasses:

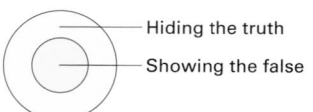

Hiding the truth
(level-one deception)
is according to Bell
and Whaley a superset
of showing the false
(level-two deception).

Hiding the truth	
	Showing the false
Masking	Mimicking
Repackaging	Inventing
Dazzling	Decoying
Bell and Whaley's classes of deception	

Deception intended to hide the truth is divided into showing the false and three subclasses: masking, repackaging, and dazzling.

• Masking means blending in with the background, for example as done with most military camouflage.

• Repackaging means redesigning the appearance to resemble something "uninteresting." Making a cannon look like a cowshed belongs in this category.

• Dazzling means confusing the spectator by making the target unclear, for example by sending messages in code or sending five messages, of which only one is true.

Deception meant to show the false is divided into mimicking, inventing, and decoying, which all aim at attracting the spectator's attention away from something which should remain unseen.

• Mimicking, like repackaging, means to take the form of something else; but the purpose of mimicking is to attract rather than avoid attention. A duck-hunter's duck decoy and a fisherman's lure belong here (not under "decoying").

• Inventing implies construction of something nonexistent. Fake vehicles, buildings, and airfields belong to this category.

• Decoying means doing something that makes the spectator look in the wrong direction. Magicians make their living by decoying.

None of Bell and Whaley's six classes seems to cover expressively our modes of overstatement and understatement. Bell and Whaley (1991, 55, 57) categorize two military instances of exaggerating the number of troops (Germany in World War I) and downplaying the number of troops (China in the Korean War) as mimicking and repackaging, respectively.

Acknowledging the differences between martial deception and pretense design and taking into consideration the importance of overstatement and understatement in the beautification field of pretense design, we shall keep our already-suggested four modes: overstatement, understatement, simulation, and hiding.

Object language
Summing up

We have just introduced a new province of design,
"pretense design," which in some way or another
misrepresents its true nature in order to impress
somebody. To enable a closer look at this intriguing
field of design inquiry, we codified pretense design in
seven dimensions, which together describe any case
of pretense design:

1. Inspired by spoken and written language,
we defined three levels of truth-bending: the
truth edited, the truth on standby, and the truth
suspended. We established that these categories are
relevant to pretense design.

Truth-bending levels

2. We looked at the motives behind pretense
design and found four possible objectives:
beautification, amusement, substitution, and
deception.

Objectives

3. We discussed the way the truth-bending
takes place in pretense design and came up with four
modes: overstatement, understatement, simulation,
and hiding.

Modes

4. We established that different kinds of
pretense design address perception and cognition in
two different ways: overtly and covertly.

Perceptibility

5. The roles are producer, pretender, and
addressee. Some of the roles may sometimes be
enacted by the same party.

Roles

6. The process of design pretense, the social
interaction, involves three communication elements.
They are medium, message, and pretense.

Communication
elements

7. Pretense design meanings are formed by
denotation and by connotation. Four combinations
exist: True denotation / false connotation; false
denotation / no connotation; false denotation / true
connotation; false denotation / false connotation.

Meanings

Interrelations between these seven dimensions exist. Beautification is, for instance, often concerned with editing the truth and with overstatement or understatement, and takes place overtly. Deception, on the other hand, is always concerned with suspending the truth, often involves fabrication, and takes place covertly.

In the following chapters we shall take a closer look at pretense design practices. We shall present a suite of pretense design examples according to their objectives: beautification, amusement, substitution, and deception, respectively. Whatever the objective, deceptive likeness is always a fundamental quality of pretense design.

Beautification

Never worry about the facts.
Just project an image to the public.
—Diana Vreeland, fashion editor (1903–1989)

Beautification
Self-presentation

The beautification discussed in this chapter deals
primarily with the enhancement of personal beauty,
which is part of a larger field known as self-
presentation. It is a euphemistic rewriting of reality.
Self-presentation—to present oneself—comprises any
behavior intended to create, modify, or maintain one's
impression in the minds of others (Brown 2007). The
basic means of self-presentation are what we say,
our manners, and our appearance, the latter including
physique, grooming, dressing, and accessorizing.
The deeper purpose of self-presentation is to show
something which otherwise would not be noticed
as easily, as soon, or at all. To self-present means to
present an edited version of oneself.

When together with other people (and
sometimes when alone), we try to present ourselves
in the most favorable light. We do this for three
specific reasons. First, we self-present to create
a pleasant situation for those involved. Good
physicians will present themselves in a certain
way to facilitate their encounter with patients: they
will be well-groomed and sober, to meet just two
reasonable expectations. Second, we self-present to
gain material or social advantages. As jobseekers,
employees, bosses, sales people, lawyers, politicians,
and in several other capacities, we want to make an
impression that will help us achieve our goals. Third,
by convincing others, we may convince ourselves.
Self-presentation can include an element of self-
motivation: we need to achieve what we say we will
achieve.

How successful we are in our self-presentation depends on our ability to "read" what is needed, but also depends on our motivation, and our willingness to deliver the needed action.

Also, the success of self-presentation relies on its desirability and believability. The qualities presented must be wanted by the audience, and they must be credible. A distinction between white lies and out-and-out lies should be observed here. It is one thing to suggest that you are younger than you are, but quite another thing to suggest that you are a physician, if you are not.

Among several strategies for self-expression we shall focus here, with a view to the subject of this chapter, on strategies where visual appearance may play a role. These are, for instance, ingratiation and self-promotion. Ingratiation means pleasing the audience by saying and doing things and looking in ways that will please. Self-promotion involves exhibiting competence in fields considered relevant. A mix of ingratiation and self-promotion is needed in many situations. As jobseekers we want to show competence but also that we are nice company. Self-promotion that is too strong can hinder ingratiation. The self-presenter's social acuity, ability to read the situation, will decide the balance between ingratiation and self-promotion.

We challenge the sometimes heard suggestions that personal appearance doesn't matter to others or to ourselves. We are all self-presenters, and we do care about our personal appearance. Personal beautification is a branch of pretense design that involves most of us, if not necessarily on a hysterical level. The beautification instances in this chapter deal with body-related issues.

Beautification
Mother of deception

It is a widespread belief that design exclusively deals with giving shape to what Germans call *Geschmackgüter,* literally "taste goods," objects in which aesthetic appearance plays a decisive role, such as fashion, cars, and decorative objects for the home. Designers resist this limitation of their field of operation: they claim that all artifacts are designed. Nevertheless, the fact remains that famous designers typically won their fame by designing beautiful objects and environments.

In affluent societies, the interest in consumption and ownership slides from quantity toward quality. When people can pay more for food, they don't eat double as much as before; instead, they eat better. Concurrent with this movement in preferences from quantity to quality, appearance plays a growing role in our experience of quality. The demand for quality moves from appreciation of technical performance toward interest in aesthetic and symbolic values.

Addressing the movement of interest and demand toward appearance, the market supply becomes sense-driven rather than technology-driven. Appearance rather than durability is the defining quality when large retail clothing companies power-advertise internationally famous models presenting ephemeral fashion at astonishingly low prices.

Eyeglasses provide one example of the slide of interest from technical function to appearance. They have developed from a medical necessity to a fashion accessory. In bygone times, spectacles were a prosthetic that helped visually impaired people to live a life with better vision. Today, the appearance of the eyeglasses is as important as their vision-enhancing function. The eyeglasses are as much to be seen with as to see with.[1]

Long ago the optometrists dropped their white coats and knitted brows. Their shops today are more fashion boutiques than anything else. The vocabulary used for eyeglasses illustrates the trajectory: spectacles, glasses, eyewear, designer frames. Not exclusive to eyeglasses, this development is seen in many object categories.

Sunglasses are still called so, but are today used, sunshine or not, indoors and outdoors. Indoors and after dark, sunglasses serve as adornment. Self-presentation has overtaken their technical function.

[1] In *The Adventures of Tom Sawyer* (1878), Mark Twain foresaw the development of eyewear from optical function to appearance when he wrote, "[The old lady's] spectacles were built for 'style' not service" (Twain 2010, 7).

Beautification
Mother of deception

Beautification becomes pretense design by hiding reality when projecting something considered more beautiful. Pretense design for beautification addresses first and foremost our personal appearance. Fragrances, makeup, hair dyes, all kinds of body-regulating lingerie, and high-heeled shoes are time-honored female staples. And men's use of illusory body scents will soon catch up with the female use, if advertising works.

Pretense design for beautification also applies to objects. A family car can be accessorized to look sportier than it is. An old car can be superficially revamped for sale. When the southern part of continental Denmark voted itself back from Germany in 1920, the erstwhile Danish King Christian X symbolically crossed the now defunct border on a white horse. Since then a rumor has kept popping up that the royal equine was painted white. Pretense design took place, or is thought to have taken place.[1]

Pretense design for beautification involves all three levels of truth-bending: the truth edited, the truth on standby, and the truth suspended. It also uses all four pretense design modes: overstatement, understatement, simulation, and hiding. Pretense design for beautification works sometimes overtly, sometimes covertly. Denotation, direct reading of the augmented beauty, delivers the meaning.

[1] A website on Danish history run by Aarhus University repeats— and rejects—the story, which they call a myth (Danmarkshistorien.dk, 2017).

13

Figure 13
Gucci magazine
advert, United
Kingdom, 2010s
Are men catching up
with women in their
use of illusory body-
scents?

Beautification
A personal matter

We carefully stage our visual presence in society and thereby take responsibility for our self-image and, to some extent, for other people's opinion about us and our role in life. Contradict thy maker, reinvent yourself, is the agenda. The mise-en-scène is to a considerable degree material and visual. It includes the ways we maintain, develop, and prettify our body, and how we dress and accessorize. Shakespeare's notion of the world as a stage is as valid as ever.[1]

Many (most?) of us regret that we have not received the looks we deserve. The choice is to accept status quo, or to take up the fight. L'Oréal's catchphrase, "Because You're Worth It" ("L'Oréal," En.wikipedia.org, 2017), recommends the latter alternative.

In *The Unfashionable Human Body*, Bernard Rudofsky suggested that people have never accepted their given appearance and early on identified room for improvement: "Uneducated and over-sophisticated alike seem to act on an uncontrollable impulse to rearrange their anatomy" (1984, 93). False nails and eyelashes (falsies) are small body supplements. The catalog of cosmetic surgery expands and so do our attitudes about what is de rigueur and what is questionable. One thing is sure: our attitude about bodily changes changes.

Whether the result of numerous intentional body modifications is a pretense or just presents reality often defies a precise answer. Rather than getting lost in philosophical dusk, we can establish that the boundaries between genuine and artificial, between true and false, nowhere are more flexible. Pretense design is fully integrated in the ways we stage ourselves.

[1] *All the world's a stage, and all the men and women merely players. They have their exits and their entrances, and one man in his time plays many parts.*
—Shakespeare 1623, *As You Like it*

Part of the personal stage setting is durable; part is ephemeral. We tend to consider durable changes more real than short-lived changes. Cosmetic surgery aims at durable changes. The man who gets his protruding ears adjusted and the woman who gets her breasts enlarged are cases in point.

Weight gained or lost and personal fitness achieved by a healthy lifestyle including physical training should hardly be considered pretense design. Those are changes of chosen reality.

For some reason or another we tend to call false hair color false, while nobody says that about red polished nails. Instead, they are called adornments. Perhaps we look at the intentions: the false blonde pretends, while the woman with red nails performs. We perceive strictly unnatural scents that nullify and replace our natural body scent in the same way we see red nails. This also applies to hair dyed in strictly unnatural colors.

The original function of clothing has long been taken for granted. Most often clothes still protect our body against climate, danger at work, and prying eyes, but the fashion industry focuses, and most money is spent, on other aspects, which to a considerable degree divert the focus from the clothing's protective qualities. Like cosmetics, clothes can serve corrective purposes. They can hide or divert attention from disliked body features and accentuate, exaggerate, or invent bodily attraction. Overstatement, understatement, simulation, and hiding may all be in play. "For the apparel oft proclaims the man," Polonius instructed his son Laertes in Shakespeare's *Hamlet* (1603, 1.3).

And of course adornment, if skilfully employed, improves; that is what it is for. The question is whether the moralists are right to imply that such improvement in personal appearance is invariably dishonest. The answer, surely, is NO. On the contrary, it can be argued that improving things—our educations, our gardens, our incomes, lives, marriages, and therefore why not our looks, and thereby our confidence?—is a good thing, even indeed a duty.
—Grayling 2010, 55

Beautification
Body paint

Painting human body parts for beautification is probably a habit as old as paint. Most visible parts of the human body, including skin, hair, eyelashes, eyebrows, eyes, lips, and nails, have served as human canvases.

In 1956, Clairol, the American manufacturer of personal-care products, introduced their highly successful slogan, "Does she … or doesn't she?," implying that nobody could tell the difference between naturally colored and Clairol-dyed hair (buildingpharmabrands 2013). Later, as mores changed and restraint gave way to whatever works, this issue became less interesting. For many years, hair color transformations have filled a continuum ranging from natural-looking shades to highly conspicuous hues. The former kind of hair dyeing both hides the truth and shows the false, and can, in principle, take place covertly. The latter variety of hair dyeing hides the truth and overtly shows the false, in that the result is obviously artificial. If the motive behind a drastic color change is fun, we will classify it as amusement; if the motive is hiding while the wearer commits a crime, we will classify it as deception.

Seen in historical perspective, Clairol was not a first mover. Since antiquity, innumerable methods have been used to dye hair. Venetian courtesans allegedly dyed their hair in horse urine and dried it in the sunshine to obtain the attractive Venetian golden-yellow.

Lips compete with eyes at being the windows of the soul. Cleopatra reportedly had her lipstick made of crushed carmine beetles (Edmonds 2011), which establishes that coloring the lips is not a modern invention.

Does she...
or doesn't she?

Hair color so natural only her hairdresser knows for sure!

That wonderfully radiant, outdoors-y look is *more* than just the reflection of a little clean air and sunshine. It's the silky sheen of her hair, its clear sparkling color that looks as fresh and natural in blazing sunlight as it does by the light of the moon. And *that's* the beautiful difference with Miss Clairol! In *every* light, finished tone is soft, ladylike... gray is completely covered. And all it takes is minutes!

That's why most hairdressers recommend Miss Clairol—use it *every* time to put lasting *young* color back into fading hair ...and to hide gray. With results so sure, why deny yourself the joy of knowing you're a younger-looking, more attractive woman! Try Miss Clairol yourself. Today. In wonderful new Creme Formula or Regular.

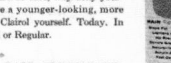 HAIR COLOR BATH®

MORE WOMEN USE MISS CLAIROL THAN ANY OTHER HAIR COLORING

14

Figure 14
Does she ... or doesn't she?
Clairol hair color ad, United States, 1957
Memorable, spot-on slogan from a time when hair dyeing was not generally accepted.

Pretense Design   69

Beautification
Body paint

In the modern world, body paint is most often applied to the female face as makeup, including lipstick, rouge, and more. But as clothes increasingly have become a matter of appearance, often at the expense of practical functions, they could in principle just as well be painted directly on the body. Indigenous people have painted directly on their skin what they could not acquire materially—for instance, imitations of British officers' uniforms (Rudofsky 1984, 137). In the Prussian army soldiers who could not grow a moustache were commandeered to paint one ("Prussian," En.wikipedia.org 2017). During World War II, women painted stockings or just stocking seams directly on their legs to emulate silk stockings (Spivack 2012). When actress Demi Moore had her body painted to pose for "Demi's Birthday Suit" on the cover of *Vanity Fair,* it was, however interesting the result, pretense for amusement rather than beautification.

Tattoos, ink under skin, appear as what they are: pure decoration. They hardly deceive anybody. Well, there are removable tattoos that look like the real thing, but offer easy repentance (pretense design!). In Japan, where tattoos were historically used to punish criminals, they are still considered stigmas and primarily sported by the mafia. Japanese gyms and public baths, for example, don't admit tattooed persons ("Irezumi," En.wikipedia.org 2017). As a main rule, tattoos are not pretense design.

Body paint used for pretense is typically read directly. Beautiful red lips denote beautiful red lips. In certain places at certain times, body paint, like painting the lips red, may connote celebrity, acting, or loose morals. The denotation is false, the connotation may be true or false.

Figure 15
Estée Lauder magazine advert, United Kingdom, 2012
Most visible parts of the human body including skin, hair, eyelashes, eyebrows, eyes, lips, and nails serve as human canvases.

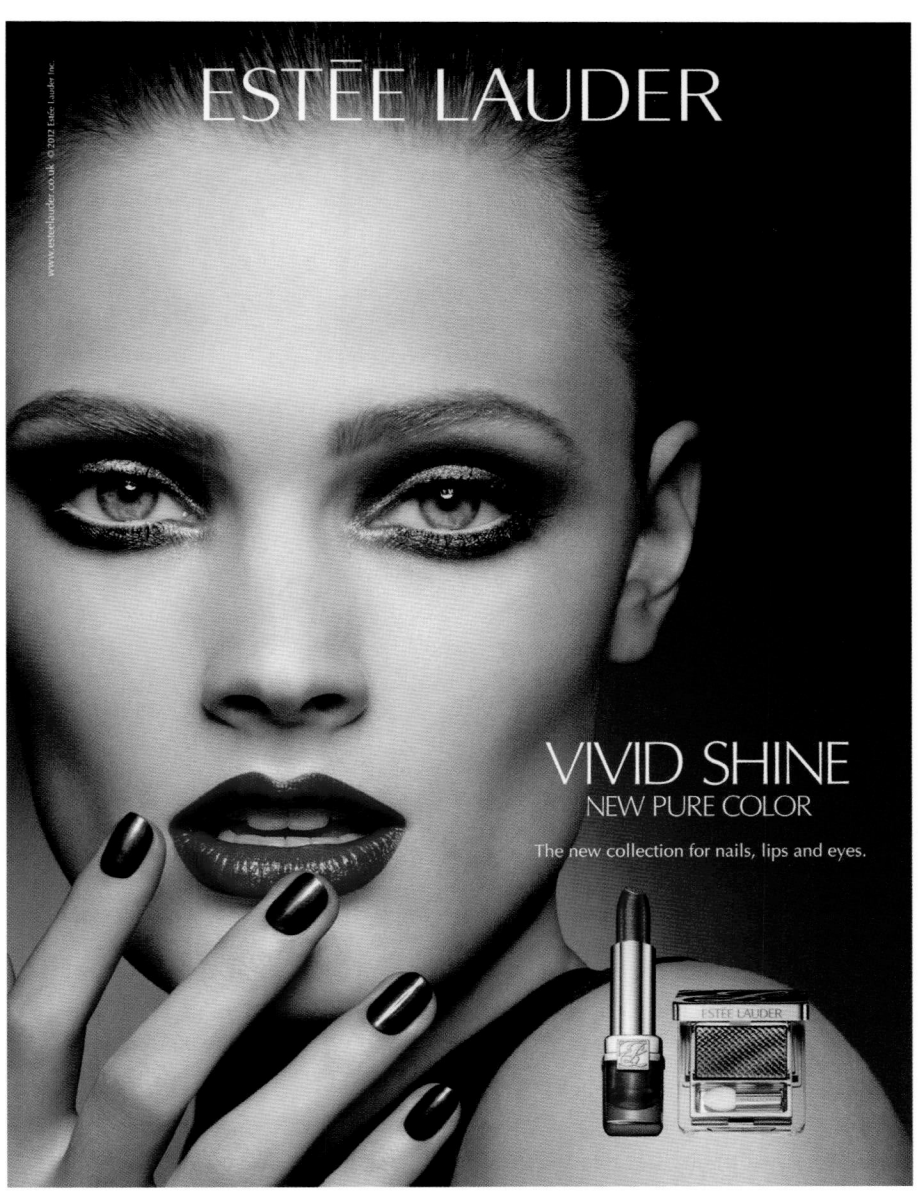

15

Considering a tan to be attractive is a relatively new phenomenon among Caucasians. For ages, a tan was a stigma of the working class. When the British upper class sailed port-out-starboard-home to the Orient, they avoided a tan as well as the heat (and possibly inspired the acronym "posh"). Nivea, the skin products brand, means literally "white as snow" in Latin. Indeed, the whitest shade of pale used to be the ideal. To keep their skin white, ladies would sport parasols or umbrellas, the latter having their etymological root in Italian umbra and Greek ombros, both meaning "shadow." Some women would apply dangerous chemicals containing lead to color their skin whiter than otherwise possible ("Sun Tanning," En.wikipedia.org 2017).

These skin color preferences allegedly changed when Coco Chanel said so in the 1920s ("Sun Tanning," En.wikipedia.org 2017), and F. Scott Fitzgerald and his crowd discovered the French Riviera to be a nice place for doing nothing in the winter. Jean Patou introduced the first sun lotion, Huile de Chaldée, in 1927 (Thefullwiki.org 2017). Since then, the affluent have seen a tan as a beautiful sign of well-being. Well, not unanimously: "there is nothing healthy about a tan" and "skin cells in trauma," warns the Australian Cancer Institute in their Dark Side of Tanning campaign, as tanning raises the risk of skin cancer, especially melanoma (Cancerinstitute.org.au 2018).

Tanning denotes a certain skin color, probably an effect of exposure to the sun. Tanning may also connote health and affluence.

Figure 16
Woman with a Parasol / Madame Monet and Her Son (La Promenade)
Claude Monet, 1875
From a time when upper-class ladies used umbrellas, long sleeves, and hats to avoid a tan.

16

Tans are not for sun-worshippers only. Sunless tanning and sunbeds are available to those who are more interested in the result than in the process.

Sunless tanning, UV-free tanning, and fake tanning refer to the application of chemicals to the body that will result in darkened skin. One benefit of this method is the absence of the dangerous ultraviolet radiation. Not so with sunbeds; their use involves ultraviolet radiation which can cause skin cancer. Dangerous or not, some people will take health risks to look healthy. Sometimes pretense design comes at a price.

What is false and what is true? Is a tan acquired under the sun more authentic than a tan acquired in a sunbed, or an instant tan fresh from an aerosol can? The tan is a tan in all three cases. The crux of the matter is the provenance. Is it nobler to sport a (dangerous) tan acquired in Saint Tropez than a (not dangerous) tan from a can, just as old money is considered better than new money?

Figure 17
Neutrogena instant bronze ad
Neutrogena, United States
Is less unhealthy sunless tanning also less attractive than traditional sun tanning?

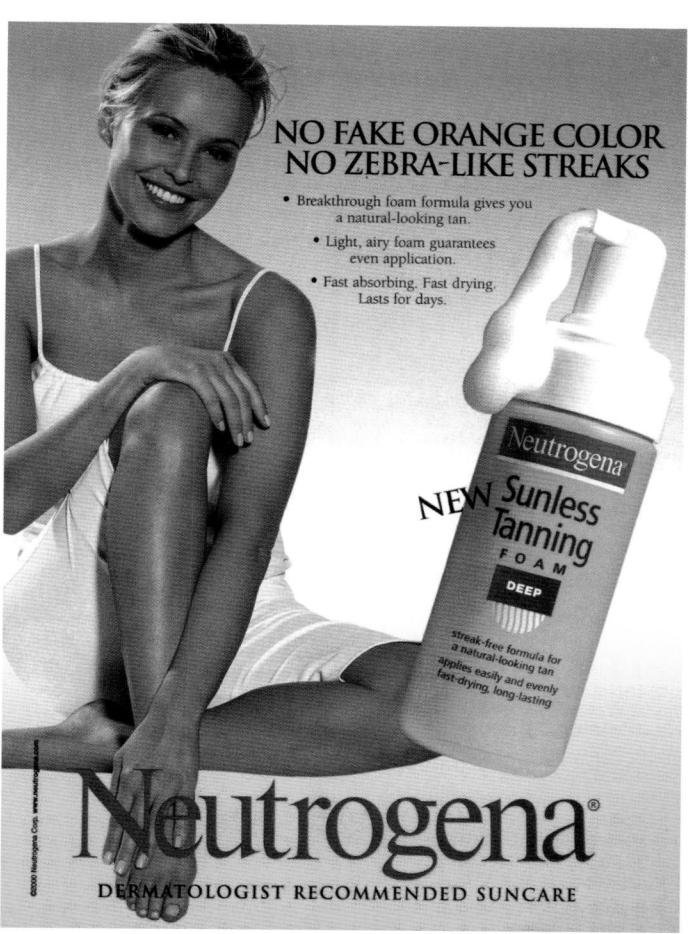

17

It is not known when high heels made their first appearance. But we do know that butchers in ancient Egypt elevated themselves by high heels to avoid wet feet, and that much later, Catherine de Medici and Mary I of England added to their height by wearing high heels ("High-Heeled," En.wikipedia.org 2017). Since then high heels for women have walked in and out of fashion. Fashion is basically about change.

In Mediterranean countries, small men habitually sport platform shoes which have thick visible soles. In contrast, elevator shoes have internal soles invisible from the outside. They are preferred by gentlemen who want to fight their vertical challenge with some discretion. Manufacturers of elevator shoes promise two or more inches' elevation by invisible soles (Tall Men Shoes 2017). Humphrey Bogart had vertical help to surpass Ingrid Bergman in height in the movie *Casablanca* (IMDb 2017).

Shoes, like most clothing, were invented for protection. Since then shoes and their taller siblings, boots, have taken on other functions. Apart from contributing their own beauty and increasing the wearer's height, high heels may expose the body in ways considered attractive. Women's high-heeled shoes make their feet look smaller and their legs appear longer and slimmer. Additionally, high heels change the wearer's posture and gait in a presumably seductive way. Super-slim tapered stiletto heels, ten centimeters and taller, constitute the high heels' formula one.

Invisible high heels denote a certain height. Visible high heels denote a certain augmented height.

I don't know who invented high heels, but all women owe him a lot.
—Marilyn Monroe, American actress (1926–1962)

**Figure 18
Poster for
Casablanca
Directed by Michael Curtiz, 1942**
Humphrey Bogart (173 cm) reportedly had artificial help to appear taller than Ingrid Bergman (175 cm).

18

Amusement

Magic does not exist. It's an illusion.

Amusement

Irrational otherness

Living in a world dominated by effectivity, rationalization, and specialization, we can easily miss something less rational. Sailing around the world, walking the Camino, and retiring into Thoreauesque woodland solitude are acknowledged breaks from the rational life, but less drastic, more temperate, answers are available. Irrational otherness is the signature quality in the amusement province of pretense design: otherness as an uproar against sameness; otherness as a flight of fantasy. Beautification always involves otherness, but it is an otherness exclusively directed toward beauty. In amusement pretense, otherness involves more than beauty; it involves meaning. The meaning comes in different shades.

Many pretense design examples dealt with in this chapter celebrate times past. They are anachronisms. For reasons other than logic, design features from bygone times are taken up for contemporary use. Old building and furniture styles are reconsidered. Functionalism is a special case: rooted in the late nineteenth and early twentieth centuries, it celebrates the aesthetic expression of function, but not necessarily functionality.

Other instances of amusement pretense refer to other places. They are anatopisms. In China, new metropolises emulate European cities, for example. Hotels in Macao and Las Vegas imitate Venice, complete with canals, gondolas, Saint Mark's Tower, and Rialto Bridge.

Adventure dominates several categories of pretense design, including intrepid chicness, wildlife trophy walls, and honorable scars.

19

Finally, some instances of amusement pretense deal with pure illusion, visual jokes. Trompe l'oeil, visual distortion, ha-has, eloquent packaging, and disguised food belong here.

In amusement pretence, functional elements are metamorphosed into something symbolically interesting.

.

Figure 19
Fruit de viande
(meat fruit)
Heston Blumenthal
English celebrity chef Heston Blumenthal likes to challenge the guests in his three-star restaurant The Fat Duck. The meat fruit, a chicken liver mousse, is created to look like a mandarin orange.

Amusement
Architecture

Architecture is a much-frequented playground for the amusement branch of pretense design. Buildings talk, and the talk is not restricted to such time-honored design themes as genesis and affordance, how the buildings are constructed, and what the buildings can be used for. The illusory themes are numerous:

- Some buildings are more or less exact copies of other buildings.

- Some buildings borrow styles from bygone periods and thereby, like small children, suggest they are older than they are. Terms such as "renaissance," "historicism," "classicism," and "revival" advertise this tendency.

- Every building has a façade that possibly hides, euphemizes, or misrepresents what is behind. This tendency is brought to its extreme in so-called façadism, aka façadomy, where the façade is left untouched when an old house is demolished and a new building is erected behind the original façade. Façadism is an adoring, if not envious, nod at history.

- Some buildings are pure charades and mimic manmade or natural objects: hotdogs, glasses, fruit, or whatever. Some buildings have forced perspective or illusory parts supplied by trompe l'oeil artists or commercial suppliers. Some buildings are covered by, or constructed of, faux materials.

American architecture is the art of covering one thing with another thing, which, if genuine, would not be desirable.
—Leopold Eideltz (quoted from Lewin 1991, 13)

Facades are found in many places, most traditionally on buildings, where they are erected to project an image that is more stylized or refined than the structure behind them.
—Burroughs 2007, n.p.

20

**Figure 20
Sainsbury Wing,
National Gallery,
London
Design: Robert
Venturi and Denise
Scott Brown, 1991**
Visual quotations
include clubhouses
on Pall Mall, the
Vatican's Scala Regia,
Victorian warehouses,
and ancient Egyptian
temples.

• Some buildings have skins that pretend to be structural but hide other, cheaper, or more functional materials. Roman builders used thin marble slats to create the illusion that houses were built of marble blocks. Today concrete buildings are often covered by a skin of bricks. Some buildings have elements that appear to be structural, but are pure decoration. Columns routinely serve in this unfunctional function.

After World War II, many damaged buildings in European cities were rebuilt to look as they had before the war. Sometimes totally destroyed buildings were rebuilt as they had been after several years of nonexistence. In Warsaw, Poland, whole historic quarters were rebuilt with help from an artist's paintings of the prewar city ("Story" 2016). Often, anastylosis—reusing the original building parts—was applied ("Warsaw," En.wikipedia.org 2017). The logic behind the rebuilding is that in the long run nobody will remember the few years of architectural absence. The line between authentic and inauthentic architecture is blurred.

Skopje, the capital of the republic of Macedonia, has gone a step further than rebuilding what once was. Following their "Skopje 2014" plan from 2010, they have renewed the central part of the city with around twenty "old" buildings and forty "old" monuments that never existed before ("Skopje," En.wikipedia.org 2018). The purpose was to give Skopje a classic look with new "old" cultural and government buildings as well as bridges. Several façades of preexisting buildings were reconstructed in an even older style.

21

While other cities commission star architects to cash in on the Bilbao effect[1] and enter the world tourist map with groundbreaking architecture, Skopje has walked in the opposite direction and commissioned a past that never was. Architectural pretense design works openly; it puts the truth on standby, works with simulation or with overstatement, and, finally, denotes something false.

[1] Named after the turnaround that the new Guggenheim Museum designed by Frank Gehry gave the city of Bilbao (Economist.com 2014).

**Figure 21
The Museum of Archaeology, Skopje, Macedonia, 2014**
A new edifice built to appear older than it is.

22

**Figure 22
Binoculars Building,
Venice, Los Angeles
Design: Frank Gehry,
2001**
The binocular part
of the three-style
building was designed
by Claes Oldenburg
and Coosje van
Bruggen.

**Figure 23
Bibliothèque
Nationale de France,
Paris
Design: Dominique
Perrault, 1995**
Four towers have the
shape of open books.

23

Columns epitomize the trajectory in architecture from functional necessity to aesthetic possibility. What was needed yesteryear becomes wanted today. That the most structural among structural elements becomes the pretense building element par excellence should not surprise; it is exactly the strong functional alibi that confers upon the column its symbolic power. However needless, columns suggest a function.

Constituting a time-honored architectural theme, columns are codified in orders, styles that include base, shaft, and capital. Doric, Ionic, and Corinthian orders originated in Greece; Tuscan and Composite orders originated in Rome.

Columns are serial pretenders. They suggest that they support something, but often support nothing but themselves. They often appear to be made of one piece of material but are built of drums, stacked on top of each other. They often appear to be of marble, but are made of concrete or wood. Sometimes, columns are anthropomorphized and take the shape of caryatids—load-bearing women—or their male counterparts, telamones (aka atlantes, the plural of atlas). Sometimes columns take the shape of animals or legendary creatures. Sometimes columns are only half-circular columns attached to a façade, or they are pilasters, half-flat columns attached to a façade.

Figure 24
The five
architectural orders
The *Encyclopédie*,
1751–1772
Top: Tuscan and Doric orders
Center: Ionic order
Bottom: Corinthian and Composite orders

Chapiteaux des cinq Ordres, avec le Chapiteau Ionique
Moderne .

Chapiteau Toscan .   Chapiteau Dorique .

2 Modules, ou 24 minutes,

Chapiteau Jonique   Chapiteau Jonique Moderne .

Chapiteau Corinthien .   Chapiteau Composite .

2 Modules, ou 36 minutes .

Benard Fecit .

24

25

26

Figure 25
The church of St-Gervais-et-St-Protais in Paris, sixteenth century
The columns represent three orders:
Third floor: Corinthian
Second floor: Ionic
Ground floor: Doric

Figure 26
Colonnade connecting Moltke's Palace with Schack's Palace Amalienborg, Copenhagen
Design: C. F. Harsdorff, 1794
The colonnade was built as an interim solution, but has remained in place. The Ionic columns were, for economic reasons, made of wood, oil-painted and treated with sand for a marmoreal appearance.

Distortion—defined as the act of giving a misleading account or impression—is a type of pretense design connected with at least two architectural principles: entasis and forced perspective.

Entasis stands for the adjustment of building elements to avoid optical illusions. In Greece and Rome, builders would widen the middle of columns to avoid straight sides that appeared concave. Sometimes they would also taper the columns toward the top to make them appear longer and (perhaps be) stronger. Very little is known about the original reasoning behind entasis, which is seen in several varieties around the world.

Forced perspective is created to adjust the appearance of a normal perspective. Forced perspective works by manipulating the sizes of building parts to make them look larger or smaller, closer or more distant, than they would appear in normal perspective. New York's Statue of Liberty has an overproportioned upper part to create a view from the ground that appears normal. When the statue was built—at the time before aviation—all viewers would see it only from the ground ("Forced," En.wikipedia.org 2017).

Forced perspective is used in architecture to create special visual effects, in the theater to save space (see p. 25), and in the film industry to save money. The four pretense design objectives— beautification, amusement, substitution, and deception—are not mutually exclusive.

The four pretense design objectives, beautification, amusement, substitution, and deception, are not mutually exclusive. Distortion as described in this section is as much a matter of beautification as of amusement.

Figure 27
Temple of Athena, Paestum, Italy, ca. 500 BCE
The columns have convex sides (entasis) and are tapered toward the top.

28

Figure 28
The Potemkin Stairs,
Odessa, Ukraine,
1841
The stairs extend for
142 meters. The width
of the stairs decreases
with the distance from
the bottom, creating
the illusion of a much
longer construction.
Sergei Eisenstein's
silent film *Battleship
Potemkin* (1925)
included a scene on
these stairs, which
later were named after
the movie.

Figures 29, 30
Forced perspective
in Roman Emperor
Constantine's Aula
Palatina, Trier,
Germany, fourth
century
The windows in the
apse are smaller than
the other windows,
to make the church
interior appear larger
than it is.

29, 30

Façadism, also known as façadomy, refers to the practice of leaving the façade untouched when demolishing an old building so it can adorn a new building. Façadism is a much-debated compromise between preservation and demolition. The practice conflicts with the Venice Charter of the International Council on Monuments and Sites ("Façadism," En.wikipedia.org 2017), and is disliked by preservationists. Local building codes, however, sometimes prescribe old skins on new buildings.

     Façadism exists in several varieties. In some cases, builders respect the original height and floor structure of the building. In other cases, a completely new building of a different height—typically higher— and a different floor structure rises behind the old façade; the façade becomes a mask. Radical façadism happens when builders transplant a façade from an old building in one location to a new building in another location.

Figure 31
Radical façadism
The University of
Melbourne, 1930s
The Old Commerce Building at the University of Melbourne includes a façade from a Melbourne bank superimposed on the front of a new campus building.

Figure 32
Hearst Tower, New York City
Design: Foster + Partners (1928) 2008
No respect shown for the building's original height.

31, 32

Amusement
Ha-ha

Nature is bigger and better than us. We fear it, and we love it. The history of civilization can be seen as one long effort to come to terms with nature. Our relation to nature has in different times and places varied from exploitation to excitement, from protection against nature to protection of nature. Agriculture, forestry, and gardening each involves edited versions of nature. The English garden, known in England as "the landscape garden," is a romanticized version of the immaculate landscape. Alexander Pope captured the idea with great precision: "True Wit is Nature to advantage dress'd" (quoted in Panofsky 1997).

Charles Bridgeman and William Kent invented the English garden in the early 1700s. Later in the same century, it was popularized by Lancelot Brown, aka Capability Brown, and since then spread to the Continent, typically on a minor scale. The English garden is a manifest expression of our split between love and fear of the wild. We want nature, but preferably in a domesticated format.

A landscape garden is an edited piece of nature framed, as a rule, by a fence. This fence, however, does not have to be visible or spoil the view. The ha-ha is a hidden fence in the shape of a trench dug in the garden or landscape. Without obstructing the view from the manor, ha-has prevent resident animals from escaping and other animals from trespassing the fenced area. Ha-has denote the nonexistence of fences. The invention of the ha-ha is often attributed to Charles Bridgeman, but it was an idea that was known previously. Ha-has exist at several country houses in England, in front of the Royal Crescent in Bath, and notably at the Washington Monument in Washington, DC.

Figure 33
Ha-ha (hidden fence in landscape garden) Castle Ashby, Northamptonshire, United Kingdom
See p. 17.

Figure 34
The ha-ha principle

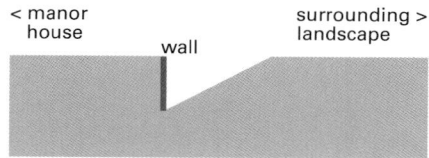

33

34

< manor
house

wall

surrounding >
landscape

Functionalism suggests that architects and designers take their point of departure from the function of the building or other object to be designed. But there is more to it.

True functionalists tend to consider their chosen style (they don't call functionalism a style) as synonymous with honesty in design. The beauty is supposed to originate directly from the functional intention, for which reason ornament is deemed *non grata*. However, it should not be forgotten that functionalism and functionality are horses of different colors. Functionalism is an -ism that cherishes function for aesthetic reasons. In fact, functionalists are, as often as not, more interested in the aesthetic expression of function than in functionality per se. Functionalism romanticizes the function and the production process by denoting overstatement.

Functionalist architects and designers have gone far to interpret functional intention. As a consequence, functionalist buildings, furniture, and other objects are typically remembered for their appearance rather than for their functional qualities. In spite of their suggestive name, the Grand Confort easy chair and sofa by Le Corbusier, Pierre Jeanneret, and Charlotte Perriand are famous for their appearance rather than for their functionality.

Some functionalists cherish visual reference to the technology used, and sometimes it is a highly idealized reference, wildly exaggerating the visible technical features. That machinelike Bauhaus chairs offer less comfortable seating than their nonfunctionalistic ancestors is one unintended result of this prioritizing.

Figures 35, 36
Functionalistic, functional, or both?

Figure 35
Wassily chair
Design: Marcel Breuer, 1925–1926
Manufacturer: Knoll, United States

Figure 36
LC2 Grand Confort
Design: Le Corbusier, Pierre Jeanneret, Charlotte Perriand, 1928
Manufacturer: Cassina, Italy

35, 36

37

**Figures 37, 38
Villa Savoye,
1929–1931
Design: Le Corbusier
and Pierre Jeanneret**
In *Towards a New
Architecture* (1923), Le
Corbusier famously
suggested: "A house
is a machine for living
in" (monoskop 2017,
4).

38

Amusement
Trompe l'oeil

Trompe l'oeil literally means "cheats the eye" in French. It is an art form in which a superrealistic painting tricks the viewer, through a friendly fraud, with a two-dimensional representation creating a lifelike illusion of three-dimensional reality.

Extreme naturalism, including perfect perspective and absence of style and personal elements, is the prerequisite of the trompe l'oeil illusion. To succeed, the trompe l'oeil artist must demonstrate his or her own absence. Much trompe l'oeil art is presented as framed paintings, where the frame breaks the illusion. Sometimes, however, the artist transcends the frame, as Pere Borrell del Caso does in his *Escaping Criticism*.

The greatest trompe l'oeil achievements are found in architecture, where trompe l'oeils suggest fictitious, scenic views, buildings, building features, and complete townscapes. Architectural trompe l'oeil was practiced in ancient Rome and probably before that in Greece. Today, trompe l'oeil paintings also serve as murals on house ends and frequently appear on wild posters covering buildings under construction or reconstruction. Used indoors, trompe l'oeils can create illusions of bookcases, fireplaces, staircases, as well as windows with interesting views. Trompe l'oeils can make small rooms bigger. They typically cost less than the real thing and they amuse. Trompe l'oeil means truth on standby. It is fabrication presented overtly. It is theater without players. Pretenders and onlookers share the joy.

39

Figure 39
Trompe l'oeil
Pere Borrell del Caso, *Escaping Criticism***, 1874**

Figure 40
Trompe l'oeil
Tullio Lombardo,
Scuola Grande di
San Marco, 1490
Venice, Italy

40

Amusement
Trompe l'oeil

41

42

Figure 41
Andrea Pozzo, fresco
with trompe l'oeil
dome painted on low
vaulting, 1703
Jesuit Church,
Vienna, Austria

Figure 42
Grand Canal
Shoppes, Venetian
Macao-Resort-Hotel,
Macao
Trompe l'oeil
used during shop
refurbishment.

Amusement
Simulacrascapes

*Baroque rhetoric, eclectic frenzy, and compulsive
imitation prevail where wealth has no history.*
—Umberto Eco (1986, 25)

China has a reputation for copying Western products
such as electronics, pharmaceuticals, and fashion.
Cases of brandmark copying in China are also known,
and recently several false Apple shops and a false
IKEA have been spotted. Originality is not necessarily
taken seriously in that country. For instance, age
is often considered more important that originality
when it comes to works of art. Chinese artists have
traditionally copied their predecessors' work to make
"old" art (Charney 2014).

     The interest in all things Western and old has
spread to whole cities in China, which are built as
more or less precise copies of European cities. What
is copied is typically a building style from the past
which long ago has been abandoned as architectural
currency in the country of origin, but certainly has
some touristic merit. The new "old" towns are
anachronisms as well as anatopisms. Hundreds of
walled and gated townships themed as Western
architecture from past periods housing millions
of people on billions of square meters surround
China's largest cities. In *Original Copies*, Bianca
Bosker (2013) has dubbed these urban developments
"simulacrascapes." Names such as Venice Water
Town, Thames Town, Holland Village, Eaton Town,
The Garden of Monet, Scandinavian Stroll, and
Weimar Villas suggest the thematic variation. The
contrast between the replaced Maoist asceticism and
the emulated bourgeois rococo, Victorian, and Beaux
Arts architecture is striking.

43

**Figure 43
Hallstatt, China**
Housing development
modeled after the
Austrian village
Hallstatt.

Amusement
Simulacrascapes

The economic boom that followed China's becoming the world's factory and the shift from command economy to market economy included a dramatic increase in income for a large part of the population and a massive move to the big cities. Both of these developments created a demand for new housing. Western-themed compounds became a conspicuous part of the answer. These new townscapes offer housing as well as the unambiguous message that the owners have arrived and possess culture.

China's themed townscapes differ in varying degrees from the originals. On the one hand, no effort is spared to include sculpture and fittings. On the other hand, scale and configuration are not always taken seriously. In Venice Water Town, buildings are eight and nine stories tall, while the Saint Mark campanile is considerably smaller than the original. Several features are changed to accommodate Chinese ideas about what Western style is or should be.

Figures 44, 45
Thames Town, China
The architecture emulates a classic British market town style.

44, 45

Amusement
Furniture reclaimed

Reproduction furniture—more or less exact copies
of furniture from former periods—covers several
period styles including renaissance, baroque, empire,
neoclassical, art deco, and Bauhaus. Some of these
material anachronisms are adorned with the official
stamp of an endorsing museum or other authority.

In the 1990s, IKEA presented a collection
of reproduced Gustavian furniture endorsed by
the Swedish National Heritage Board (IKEA 1993).
Gustavian is a specific Swedish style from the late
eighteenth and early nineteenth centuries, inspired
first by French rococo and neoclassicism and later by
engravings found in the excavations of Herculaneum
and Pompeii. Gustavian furniture was a kind of
pretense design right from the beginning. Copied
today, it is second-order pretense design; it looks like
something that looked like something.

The IKEA collection of new "old" Gustavian
furniture included replicas of a great number of
furniture items and decorative objects found at
Swedish castles, manor houses, and a health resort.
At the presentation, IKEA declared that the IKEA
Gustavian furniture was easy to distinguish from the
original furniture, since it was new, not feigning wear
and tear (IKEA 1993). (Later, the Swedish furniture
company Move Möbler took over the collection.)

Reproduction furniture sold as reproduction
furniture is theater. Amusement is the purpose.
Amusement pretense is always innocent since the
addressee is a beneficiary, not a victim. The truth is
on standby. However, reproduction furniture sold as
original is intentional crime. Buyers are deceived to
their disadvantage.

Figure 46
Reproduced
Gustavian chair
Medevi Brunn,
Sweden, 1997
Manufacturer: Move
Möbler, Sweden
The original chair
was found at Medevi
Brunn, a former
Swedish health resort.

46

Poker players bluff when they pretend to have stronger cards than they actually have. Players in contemporary life bluff when sporting highly functional clothes and other gear because of their symbolic value rather than because of an honest need of the technical function. The highly functional gear supposedly signals personal strength. The rationale is swifter, stronger, rougher—an apropos update of the Olympic motto: faster, higher, stronger. The talking gear includes clothes and accessories worn more or less close to the body, as well as vehicles and sport requisites. Intrepid chic bluffers appropriate professional, sometimes ultrafunctional, gear, sometimes in full seriousness, sometimes tongue-in-cheek. Mimetic ownership is the means, intrepid chic appearance is the end.

Men's watches with the connotation of being intrepid illustrate this trend. Some professions have special need for timekeeping. In 1904, French jeweller Louis Cartier created one of the world's first wristwatches for Brazilian aviator Alberto Santos-Dumont, who wanted to read the time without being diverted from aviating. The watch was eponymously named "Cartier Santos-Dumont." Since then, several watch manufacturers developed aviator watches, first as highly functional timekeepers for aviators, and later as male jewelry. "What are you made of?" asks a TAG Heuer watch ad featuring Brad Pitt. Early aviator watches had easily readable dials and large winding crowns to facilitate operation with gloved hands. The intrepid chic watches denote technical device and time, and connote a reckless owner. The denotation of functional equipment is complemented by the connotation of recklessness. What the audience thinks is as important as what the audience sees.

47

Figure 47
Yellow gold, pink gold
One sapphire cabochon
Cartier Santos-Dumont watch, Cartier, Paris, 1912
Manufacturer: Cartier, France
The progenitor of all aviator watches did not look like the aviator watches of today, but it was used for flying. In contrast, most modern aviator watches have circular dials and large, easily readable, upright Arabic numerals. Cartier Santos-Dumont is today marketed in several varieties, some in precious metals.

48

Figure 48
Die Grosse
Fliegeruhr, B-Uhr,
1940s
Manufacturer: IWC,
Switzerland
Official Luftwaffe
Observers Watch
from World War
II. Ø 55 mm.
Unsurpassable
intrepid chicness.
Circular dial, large
Arabic numerals, and
winding crown.

Amusement
Intrepid chic

Divers, like aviators, have special needs for keeping an eye on the time. Apart from being waterproof at great depths, their watches must have a certain size for visibility and provide extra information for personal safety in deep water. Such watches tend to be quite macho in their appearance, and have long since served as gentlemen's jewelry. Today, owners who cannot swim may outnumber professional divers wearing Rolex Submariners. Real divers wear their watch outside their wetsuit. Landlubbers in business suits emulate them.

Boat shoes with no-slip soles used ashore, and sweaters and coats with gun patches, are other props in the swifter, stronger, rougher game. Boat shoes negotiate life on the deck in wet weather and connote sailor when used out of marine context. Gun patches on sweaters and coats that were invented to prevent the rifle butt from slipping tell their own easily read stories.

Intrepid chic design represents an interesting variety of participatory design where the professional designer and the user work together and share responsibility for the result. Here the product designed by the designer combined with the way the user presents it makes it pretense design. Sometimes the product is born as pretense design; sometimes it only becomes pretense design when used in a certain way. The producer, pretender, and addressee roles may be distributed in different ways.

Why now? In a time when more and more of us spend our working life indoors rather than outdoors and use our brains rather than our body, many feel an urge to compensate physically with extreme sports and symbolically with expressive clothes and accessories.

Figure 49
Rolex Oyster Perpetual Sea-Dweller DEEPSEA

Figure 50
Boat shoes
Boat shoes, aka deck shoes, of canvas or leather and with special grip soles are worn by sailors and landlubbers alike. Boat shoes repel water and provide good grip on a wet deck. Paul Sperry invented the modern type of boat shoes with a deep pattern in the soles after having noticed how well dogs run over ice. Boat shoes have for many years been fashionable storytellers ashore ("Boat," En.wikipedia. org 2017).

49

50

Amusement
Intrepid chic

In road cycling and other popular spectator sports, the athletes' clothes double as portable advertising billboards. Amateur cyclists who take their sport seriously buy the professional gear for its function and appearance. They acquire jerseys and shorts complete with advertising. The amateurs pay to look like the professionals, who get paid.

British top model Kate Moss famously sported green Hunter wellies and inspired a generation of would-be fashionistas. They dry-walk these highly functional gumboots designed for walking in the rain because of the tongue-in-cheek symbolic value.

Cars are perfect toys for playing swifter, stronger, rougher. The intrepid automotive vocabulary is rich. Spoilers, sports alloy wheels, bull bars with double antennas, snorkel exhausts, and pulleys tell owners and others their easily read stories. One genre is about speed; another is about negotiating rough terrain. The original, functionally required implements have become fashion statements.

Overstatement of functional features is not restricted to consumer goods, nor to our time. When large funnels on ocean liners were seen as signs of power and speed, shipyards would equip boats needing only three functional funnels, for example RMS *Titanic* (1911–1912), with a fourth funnel. The extra, functionally unnecessary funnel on four-funnel liners (aka four-stackers) was empty or used for other purposes.

Figure 51
Jeep
Manufacturer:
Chrysler, United
States
Four-wheel driving is an all-year passion.

51

52

Figure 52
Amateur bicyclists
Advertising
jerseys show your
professionalism.

53

**Figure 53
RMS *Titanic* (1911–
1912) and her sister
ship, RMS *Olympic*
(1911–1935)**
On both four-funnel
liners, the fourth
funnel was a dummy.
(RMS = Royal Mail
Ship.)

Skeuomorphism

A skeuomorph is an artifact adorned with technical features characteristic in design of previous periods which are no longer needed. The word "skeuomorph" derives from Greek: skeuos = vessel or implement, morphe = form. A plastic table with a wood grain pattern is a skeuomorph, as are the church chandelier's electric bulbs that emulate candle flames. The intention behind skeuomorphism is to make the new design look familiar by emulating the appearance of yesteryear's technology. Opinions are divided: some find skeuomorphism distasteful, others find it user-friendly and funny.

Defenders of skeuomorphs on computer screens, such as Apple's old trash can icon on Mac computers, point at the indicative function of explaining the new technology by using an image of the old technology. iPhones used to sport several skeuomorphs, including a clock icon showing an analog clock, a bookshelf referring to the newsstand, a yellow legal pad indicating where to type notes, and green felt boards illustrating gaming. Apple has already abandoned some of these anachronisms which served as visual metaphors.

Skeuomorphs denote past technology and connote present function.

54

Figures 54, 55, 56, 57
Skeuomorphs with indicative function
Old technologies are shown to explain new technologies.

Figure 54
Mac trash can icon

Figures 55, 56, 57
iPhone with skeuomorphic icons

55, 56, 57

**Figure 58
Burberry ad, 1916
Burberry, United
Kingdom**
Trench coats were
invented in the
nineteenth century
and got their name
and popularity from
officers' wearing them
in the Great War. After
the war, the trench
coat got a civilian
career, but kept
its now-redundant
features such as
shoulder straps and
D-rings in the belt.

58

The way we dress includes several instances of purely ornamental skeuomorphs—originally functional features which are not needed any more, neither for physical function nor for explanation. Often we don't remember, or even think of, the origin of wanted rather than needed features.

Today, nobody takes a trench coat into a trench. The name, the shoulder straps for rank insignia, and the D-rings in the belt for map cases and other equipment survive from their military use in World War I when trench coats were worn in trenches. The trench coats were optional and for officers only. After the war, officers would keep their "trench-warms" and use them in civilian life. Today, trench coats are still marketed with a number of now-redundant functional features.

Brogues, the Scottish/Irish type of outdoor shoes, where perforations of the leather allow water to drain when used in bogs and other wet areas, have moved on to dry and more prestigious use. Gumboots have taken over the function of walking in wet conditions.

In the 1930s, several US car makers took up a coach work tradition and used wood for structural purpose in the car's rear bodywork. British manufacturers followed suit. British Motor Corporation's Morris Minor Traveller (1953–1971) was the last true mass-produced "woodie." Later, car manufacturers would add wood structure for decorative purposes only, and still later they would replace the wood structure by lookalike vinyl, something that looks like something that looked like something.

59

Figure 59
Morris Minor
Traveller, 1953–1971
Manufacturer:
British Motor
Corporation, United
Kingdom
Station car with
wooden coachwork.
The last mass-
produced woodie.

60

**Figure 60
Chrysler LeBaron
Town & Country,
1986
Manufacturer:
Chrysler, United
States**
Station wagon with
faux wooden panels

61

62

Figure 61
Brogues
Originally designed
for work in wet areas;
since then reassigned
to new functions.

Figure 62
Wire wheel cover on
a 1967 AMC Marlin
Manufacturer:
American Motors
Corporation, United
States

Amusement
Fauxthenticity

Faux is French for "false." In English, the term is often used as a euphemism that makes the false appear acceptable or even attractive. *Faux marbre*, imitated marble, and its sibling *faux bois*, imitated wood, are not derogatory terms; they denote qualities in their own right. "Fauxthenticity," a portmanteau of "faux" and "authenticity," stands for the results of making something false appear true. The term, coined by Douglas Hofstadter and Emmanuel Sander (2013), captures the essence of pretense design. Faux furs and artificial leather are other instances of fauxthenticity. The business thinking behind fauxthenticity is to combine the best of two worlds—something that is interesting but unprofitable combined with something that is cheaply manufactured but uninteresting (Hofstadter and Sander 2013).

In its widest sense, fauxthenticity includes most of the examples given in *Pretense Design* since they show the false at the expense of the true. What distinguishes the examples in this section is the extra effort taken to connote authenticity.

One of a legion of examples of fauxthenticity is computer fonts that emulate handwriting and are randomized to let the letterforms vary—made sloppier than needed—to appear to be authentic handwriting. Writing letters by hand is time-demanding, but machine-produced letters are impersonal. Mechanical perfection is sacrificed for "honest" appearance. Ceramists and other craftsmen sometimes use similar methods to denote artistic handwork. Fauxthenticity is all about denotation of the false.

Ken Robinson, an international authority on education and creativity, writes about his visit to the Venetian Hotel in Las Vegas,

> which is a huge place and includes, on the second floor, an indoor replica of San Marco's Square in Venice, complete with the Grand Canal, gondolas and gondoliers. I have been to Venice, and in some ways the Venetian Hotel is better. It's more authentic [sic] I feel, and it doesn't smell of sewage. (Robinson 2011, 119)

How authentic can fauxthenticity become?

Figure 63
The Venetian, Macao (Sister hotel to the Venetian in Las Vegas)
The water in the canal is dead calm, only accentuated by a slowly advancing gondola, heralded by the gondolier's song. This is not Venice. It is Grand Canal Shoppes, a third-floor shopping center at the Venetian Macao-Resort-Hotel in Macao, China. Guests arriving at the world's largest casino and three thousand hotel suites are welcomed by replicas of Saint Mark's Tower and the Rialto Bridge, which conveniently are located next to each other. An escalator adorns Saint Mark's Tower.

63

Steampunk is second-order fantasy: fantasy about fantasy. Steampunk expresses our time's fantasies about the Victorian era's fantasies about the future. Steampunk is a retro vision of an imagined future based on 1900 technology, Jules Vernesque images of a highly technical future. Steampunk is obsessed by the aesthetic expression of futuristic technique. It is a functionalistic caricature. Originally a literary subgenre of science fiction, steampunk has today found its material expression in interiors, clothing, and other product categories including computer keyboards and guitars.

To mark the 1994 bicentenary of the nearby Conservatoire National des Arts et Métiers, the Paris Metro station called Arts et Métiers was redesigned in true steampunk ("Steampunk," En.wikipedia.org 2017). The new station features exaggerated, unnecessary, and only apparently functional, technical features—a vision of the future in the past.

Paul St. George's Telectroscope installation at London City Hall in 2008 mimics a never-realized invention of a device that could send and receive pictures wirelessly at a distance ("Steampunk," En.wikipedia.org 2017). The installation was celebrated with interactive video installations linking London with Brooklyn, New York—new technology disguised in a fantasy about a fantasy.

64

Figure 64
Steampunk Metro
station Arts et
Métiers, Paris
Design: François
Schuiten, 1994

Amusement
Steampunk

65

Figure 65
Steampunk
Telectroscope
installation at
London City Hall
Design: Paul St.
George, 2008

Amusement
New patina

One interesting province of fauxthenticity is the pretense of patina in new products. Why do manufacturers let products look older than they are? To understand this, a peek into the symbolic meaning of patina in earlier times may prove useful.

Much in line with the general theme of *Pretense Design*, patina is a surface phenomenon, a physical and a symbolic property. Patina is the change of product surface due to age and use. Change of color, scratches, wear, and damage inform observers that the object isn't new. In most situations today, this is a regrettable fact which sellers of secondhand goods will try to downplay if it's not possible to disguise. Another option—attack is the best form of defense—is to euphemize the secondhand status as "vintage," "pre-owned," "pre-loved," or "experienced": a vintage ladies' handbag or a pre-loved Rolex Sea-Dweller.

Patina has not always been something to hide. On the contrary. In the seventeenth century, before fashion and consumerism took command, the patina of valuable belongings would be a sign of status. Rich families would pass belongings down through generations as heirlooms. The older the objects, the better proof of longstanding ownership, meaning an old lineage. Ancientness was the desired quality of riches. Patina served as a gatekeeper protecting the few from the many. As one scholar has pointed out, the patina did not prove value, for instance of a silver dish; instead, patina authenticated the value (McCracken 1990).

Amusement
New patina

The present-day artificial aging of products for sale is a horse of another, but not completely different, color. The new patina is not necessarily part of valuable items, and it carries meanings different from inherited ownership. The meanings can be just age, recklessness, or a nonchalant we-don't-care quality.

The "shabby chic" trend in interior decorating is a case in point. The term was coined by the *World of Interiors* magazine in the 1980s ("Shabby," En.wikipedia.org 2017). Visibly old and worn furniture fills the bill, but so does new, presumably cheap furniture artificially aged, painted several times before the paint is partly scraped or sanded off to make the furniture appear older (more attractive) than it is. The shabby chic label has also been applied to textiles, especially linen, as well as to gardening. The intention has been a romanticized (and unwarranted) view of yesteryear. The flowery patterns that share the label stress the romantic view.

In clothing, some denims are stonewashed or pretreated in ways that make them appear old and worn right from the beginning (stonewashed denims admittedly are softer and more pleasant in use than the real thing). Rejection of bourgeois standards is the unequivocal message. Add to this the antibourgeois message flashed by rock bands and their audiences. Denotation is complemented by connotation. New, ripped jeans with holes in the legs take this fauxthenticity one step further; they have the same level of authenticity as fencing scars achieved without fencing (see p. 142). To resemble real antiques, false antiques are sometimes "distressed" by various rough treatment as well as adorned with false wood worm holes.

Figure 66
Ripped jeans
Manufacturer:
Citizens of
Humanity, United
States

66

Amusement
Eloquent packaging

In its basic form, packaging serves several physical functions including isolating, apportioning, and protecting individual quantities of merchandise. In its modern form, packaging has, like many other designed objects, made the journey from a physical to a communicative function. The packaging must still isolate, apportion, and protect, but it must also replace the silver-tongued salesman of bygone days. The packaging must talk. Successful eloquent packaging commands attention, identifies, seduces, and forms habits. It is shelf good and home good. It stands out among competing products in the marketplace, calls for attention, says what to expect, persuades customers to buy, and later, after use, to repeat buying.

Apart from informing about content and use, packaging rhetoric can include elements of dressing up, disguise, and confusion.

Dressing up takes place when a kilo of ordinary potatoes dresses above its class in an upmarket paper bag with string closure and a little window allowing one to see the produce inside. Clothes make the man; packaging makes the merchandise.

Disguised packaging comprises a merry class of containers that look like something that they are not: wine bottles shaped like fish or bunches of grapes, honey bottles shaped like small bears or maple leaves, and containers of mouthwash camouflaged as big teeth. These packages fool nobody, but amuse many. Delightful denotation.

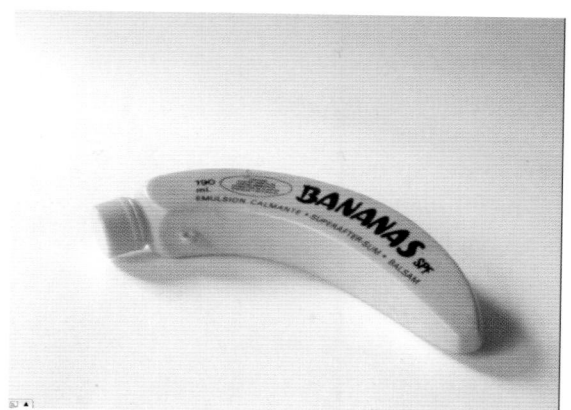

**Figures 67, 68, 69
A packaging fancy-dress party**
Bunch of grapes
contains wine;
banana: sun lotion;
lime: juice

67, 68, 69

Amusement
Trophies

Trophies are material evidence. They document where the owners have been or what they have achieved. The word "trophy" reminds us of a studio with walls covered by antlered heads of—often dangerous, sometimes endangered—exotic species. In the outset, trophies were a side effect, something secondary to the useful materials sought for and the joy of hunting. However, trophies tend to become ends in their own right. When this happens, the hunter becomes a gatherer, a collector who shoots to embellish his studio with trophies.

Trophies also exist on a less dramatic, and not wildlife-threatening, level. Luggage labels from hotels and ocean liners were originally designed for practical functions, but had the side effect of giving status, and became collectors' items in their own right. As time went by, the bragging function, I have been there, took the upper hand.

When the European borders opened after World War II, automotive holidaymakers adorned their windscreens with stickers from Grossglockner Hochalpenstrasse and other locales of touristic interest. The principle was the same as when fighter aces paint marks on the fuselage when they have downed enemy aircraft: I have been there. I have achieved.

Power brand shopping bags are small-scale urban trophies. While only few can see where you shop and what you buy, many can read your Prada, Dior, Chanel, or Armani trophy bag. Power brand shopping bags are win-win deals: the shops as well as the shoppers get exposure.

70

Figure 70
Trophy wall

All these types of trophies are expressions of nostalgia and perhaps honest bragging—as long as they are authentic. However, false regiment ties, trophies acquired without justification, perhaps brought in by the decorator, and power brand bags reused for showing off when doing less expensive shopping are instances of pretense. The user is the pretender.

In the nineteenth century and well into the twentieth, dueling among German students took a communication turn. A *Schmiss*, a grim fencing scar on the chin, became the decisive proof of courage, and the ticket to status ("Schmiss," De.wikipedia.org 2017). The scar, not the duel, became the main issue. Students with more money than courage would pay a surgeon to damage their face, and high achievers would obstruct the healing of their made-to-demand "badge of honor" scar to show off more courage. Denotation: fighting scar; connotation: honor.

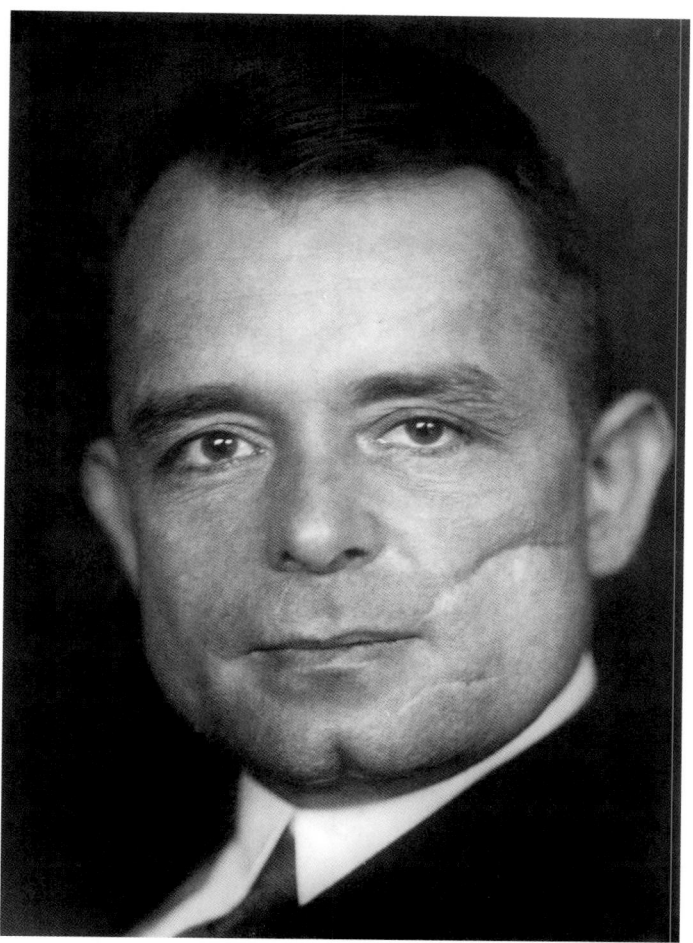

71

Figure 71
Otto Klepper,
Prussian Minister of
Finance, 1931, with
Schmiss **(honorable**
scar)

Amusement
Adventurous clothing

While we cannot decide to whom and when we are born, and can choose only to a limited degree who we are, we can hide or contradict these facts by the way we dress. Clothes are the cloth many dreams are realized by. While transvestites, impersonators, and carnival participants plunge into a full Monty,[1] most people realize their dreams on a more temperate level, helped by alert businesses. Banana Republic (1978–1983) was such a dedicated adventurous clothing supplier.

Banana Republic was a US chain of clothing shops known for their traveler clothes, their entertaining catalogs, and their thematic shop interiors. The shops were decorated with palms, taxidermied wild animals, Jeeps, and crash-landed aircraft. Banana Republic was conceived, founded, owned, and operated by husband and wife Mel and Patricia Ziegler, a journalist and an illustrator, respectively, both compulsive travelers (Ziegler 1986).

Banana Republic was a showcase of storytelling. Old world travelers to Africa and the Orient inspired the merchandise. The assortment was colorfully described by Patricia Ziegler's illustrations and Mel Ziegler's prose in catalogs that today are sold on eBay as collectors' items. The catalogs celebrate the clothes of old world colonial masters and mythical travelers.

[1] Apropos Monty: In Denmark, after World War II, a boy's military-inspired clothing was called a "Monty dress." The author sported one.

Figure 72
Banana Republic catalogue spread

Banana Republic's sources of inspiration and
emulation included Lord Kitchener, Rudyard Kipling,
Karen Blixen, Charles Lindbergh, Douglas MacArthur,
and Ernest Hemingway, as well as fictive personae
such as Ilse Lund, Rick Blaine, and Indiana Jones,
enacted by Ingrid Bergman, Humphrey Bogart,
and Harrison Ford, respectively. The icons were
represented by authentic photos and accompanied
by pictures of their clothes, now reproduced and
commercially available for anybody bent on look-alike
dressing. The catalogs were irresistible invitations to
voyages in nostalgia.

The Lone Eagle:
Charles Lindbergh,
in leather flight
helmet.

American fashion icon Ralph Lauren offers a different type of adventurous clothing and venues, transporting his well-heeled clientele to bygone times amid a shamelessly wealthy ambience. His style has been referred to as "old money classicism."

In *Ralph Lauren* (Lauren 2007), a mammoth coffee table book compiled to celebrate his first forty years in business, Ralph Lauren admits his veneration for tradition, whether that of American Ivy League universities such as Princeton, Yale, and Harvard or of old England. Lauren equates "classic" with "timeless," with a somewhat parochial view on time.

Lauren also stresses his fascination with clothes that were designed for a purpose—work clothes, uniforms, and the utility fabrics they were made of—explaining, "They have an integrity to them" (2007, 29). Lauren gentrifies work clothes and resurrects their functional features as decorative motifs. The workers whose work clothes supplied the inspiration won't complain; they don't belong to Ralph Lauren's market segment, either economically or culturally.

In terms of branding, Lauren walks the talk. His flagship shops, decorated in manor house style, and the carefully released peeps into his private life with lots of beauty are invitations to dreamland.

73

**Figure 73
Ralph Lauren
magazine advert**
Lauren's fascination
with work clothes
translated as high-
end, tongue-in-cheek,
intrepid chic.

Amusement
Travels in time, space, and fantasy

Leisure time is time for travel in time, space, and fantasy. Serious museums and an alert tourist industry understand our need for transcendence and offer attractions that teleport millions of visitors to other times and spaces.

Culture museums are time pockets of varying illusory power. Old-fashioned collections, eclectic *Wunderkammern*, or ordinary museums leave the imaginary journey to the spectators' fantasy. Not so with London's War Rooms, scores of open-air museums, and hundreds of deceased celebrities' homes. These venues manifestly send visitors back in time.

Other attractions are anatopic rather than anachronistic; they work in space rather than time and bring the exotic close to the visitor. Such attractions most often deal with water in one state or another: zoos; aquariums; dolphinaria; indoor water lands complete with waves, sand, and palm trees; rainforests; indoor or outdoor skating rinks; and indoor Alpine skiing facilities.

Disney venues and other theme parks cut the mooring to reality, transporting guests directly to the kingdom of fantasy: "Here you leave today and enter the world of yesterday, tomorrow and fantasy," reads a plaque at the entrance of Disneyland Park, Los Angeles (Bricker 2017).

74

**Figure 74
Aquadome in
Lalandia, Billund,
Denmark**
Aquadome is
the center of the
tropical water fun
land Lalandia near
Legoland in Billund.
The Aquadome offers
7,400 square meters
of heated pools
complete with waves
and water slides.
An older Lalandia is
located on the island
of Lolland, which
has the Latin name
Lalandia.

Substitution

The most successful people are those who are good at Plan B.
—James A. Yorke, mathematician (1941–)

Substitution
Second choice

When naming this category of pretense design, we chose between "ersatz" and "substitution." *Ersatz* is the German word for "replacement." It is a noun. In English the word is used as an adjective, as in "ersatz coffee." But there is another difference. In German the word *Ersatz* (uppercase initial letter) has a neutral connotation, while the word "ersatz" (lowercase) in English is pejorative. Because we file in this category several items that should not be disparaged, e.g. prosthetics, we have instead chosen the neutral "substitution" as the category label.

In our exposition, "substitution" refers to materials and objects that are used instead of other materials and other objects that would be the natural choice. The substitute pretends to be the natural thing. Substitution is about using plan B because Plan A was abandoned. The natural choice may not be available, or it may be too expensive, or just impractical. Substitution materials and objects replace something against which they will always be benchmarked. Margarine replaces butter; butter is the real thing. When we consume margarine, we compare it with butter. Likeness is the sought-after quality in substitution, although perfect likeness is not possible. If the substitute is identical with the substituted, it is not a substitute.

Substitution materials and objects are me-toos. Numerous materials were introduced to replace other materials. Wallpaper was invented to substitute for textiles, plastic laminate was invented to substitute for wood, and Corian was invented to substitute for marble. Veneering furniture is a marriage of convenience between decorative surfaces and low costs; it may also imply practical advantages.

With noteworthy exceptions such as nylons (the word is derived from "New York" + "London"), the rule is that the substitute, if identified as such, is considered at least in some way to be poorer than what is being replaced. That is also the case for faux furs, aka fake furs and fun furs (see p. 40). Artificial furs when recognized as such don't signal status, and they don't prevent snow from melting and freezing and becoming ice in the same way that animal furs do (for instance on parka trimmings). However, faux furs do have some merits, the most obvious being that they don't imply animal cruelty and killing and don't inspire special fur farms. Another advantage is that faux fur is easier to sew than real fur. Finally, there is an amusement aspect, reflected in the term "fun fur." Paradoxically, the low value is also an asset worth something.

Sometimes the substitute outperforms the substituted material or object. Nylons, originally invented to replace expensive silk stockings, have already been mentioned. When such successful replacement happens, we will tend to forget the origin and stop considering the substitute a substitute; it becomes something in its own right, the new real thing, while the substituted product may fade into oblivion. Today, leather is in Scandinavia sometimes, half-jokingly, called "wild plastic," while artificial leather, sometimes vegan leather, takes over.

Substitution
Second choice

      Prosthetics, or artificial body parts, are substitutes that hardly will be preferred to the original parts, but are nevertheless much appreciated both as a practical help and as a means to avoid stigmatization. Sometimes prosthetics outperform the substituted organ in some respects. The inventory of artificial body parts includes hair, lenses, teeth, limbs, hips, knees, windpipes (Miodownik 2014). Teeth are the most frequent artificial body parts, most often as pieces used to rebuild a damaged tooth but also as removable partial or complete dentures.

      Pornography, sailor's mate inflatable dolls, plastic genitals, and other more or less imaginative sex-related implements address the special demands of perhaps not so special constituencies.

      As a pretense design category, substitution can be *bona fide* or *mala fide*. The truth is on standby in the first case and suspended in the second case. Rhinestones sold as diamonds, and cultured pearls sold as natural pearls are mala fide substitution.

      Substitutes denote the substituted (false). That's their purpose. Substitutes may connote in the same way as the substituted would connote.

Substitution
Surface surrogates

Surfaces surround us wherever we go. Some surfaces are nothing but the outermost part of a substance. Other surfaces are front layers that differ from what they cover. A table top of solid wood belongs to the first category; when covered with veneer or plastic laminate, it enters the second category.

Designers use plastic laminate for several reasons, including its being available and cheap, and possessing attractive practical qualities. Plastic laminate's aesthetic versatility, including its capability to imitate any material, natural or manmade, is another reason for its popular use. The latter feature is what interests us here: substitution used for pretense, appearance without being.

Formica, formerly an American brand and now a New Zealand one, is to many a synonym for plastic laminate. Formica plastic laminate is made of resin-impregnated kraft paper topped with layers of printed or solid color decor and, finally, given a melamine protective layer. Originally invented as an insulating material, plastic laminate was introduced as a material for interior decoration in the late 1920s (Lewin 1991).

In the following decades, plastic laminate became synonymous with modern times. Easy cleaning, heat resistance, and hard wear combined with its versatile pattern potential, including its ability to imitate, were Formica's unique selling propositions.

We used to associate this formerly truly American surface material with kitchens and diners, the vernacular, prefabricated North American restaurants shaped as train dining cars. However, its applications are countless.

The distinction between natural and synthetic substances, just like that between traditional colours and bright colours, is strictly a value judgement. Objectively, substances are simply what they are: there is no such thing as true or false, a natural or artificial substance.
—Baudrillard 1968, 38

In the end, the inherited nobility of any given material can exist only for a cultural ideology analogous to that of the aristocratic myth itself in the social world—and even that cultural prejudice is vulnerable to the passage of time.
—Baudrillard 1968, 39

Substitution
Surface surrogates

Plastic laminates can be made to appear as faux wood, faux stone, or faux textile, or in any other natural or manmade pattern. Many designers despise plastic laminate for exactly this lookalike potential. It is not honest, they feel. Sometimes they spread these feelings to the whole idea of plastic laminate synonymous with Formica. More temperate minds embrace plastic laminate for its functional qualities.

In the 1970s, Ettore Sottsass and his Memphis Group in Milan designed a range of furniture using laminates from Formica's Italian competitor, Abet Laminati, and bestowed new design credibility upon the genre. The Memphis Group did not use plastic laminate for pretense; on the contrary, they flashed the idea of bad taste as a postmodern statement. Scores of other furniture designers, including Achille Castiglioni, Arne Jacobsen, Dieter Rams, and Jørn Utzon, have chosen to use plastic laminate for table tops because of its practical qualities as well as its no-nonsense appearance.

While the denotation of plastic laminate is straightforward—an oak pattern says oak wood, for example—the connotation may deal with the wood pattern as well as with plastic laminate as such: oak laminate panels in a pub may to some patrons connote old English pub, while to others they may connote cheap plastic atmosphere.

Figure 75
Formica plastic laminate samples: Flint Crystal, Jamocha Granite, and Metro Wood Manufacturer: Formica, New Zealand
The ability to imitate is plastic laminate's often-debated signature quality.

75

Substitution
Surface surrogates

Carbon fiber–reinforced polymer, aka CFRP, or just carbon fiber, is a strong, rigid, and lightweight composite material. It is used in aircraft, automobiles, sports equipment, and several other product categories where the combination of light weight, strength, and rigidity is needed. Carbon fiber–reinforced polymer comes in many compositions, but consists basically of carbon fiber and a matrix of polymer. Carbon fiber–reinforced polymer is fairly expensive to produce.

While originally developed and applied for its structural qualities, carbon fiber–reinforced polymer is today also used for prestigious trim on upmarket automobiles. This is beautification on par with landlubbers' boat shoes and must be classified as pretense design for amusement. As there are no great structural demands on automobile trims, cheaper lookalike materials have been called in to substitute for the "real thing," which was not so real since carbon fiber–reinforced polymer is not needed in, for example, an otherwise honest Tesla built of aluminum. Plates of fake carbon fiber are available everywhere. YouTube offers DIY instructions. A late development is that some users of the real thing allegedly cover it with a layer of paint—to avoid showing off, which is also pretense!

Diamond plates or checker plates are metal plates of steel or aluminum with a raised pattern on one side and flat on the other. The raised pattern makes checker plate a stable surface for floors or stairs in industrial or maritime settings. If used for its symbolic quality only, it could just as well be replaced by adhesive plastic sheets that simulate diamond plate and are available at building supply stores.

Inevitably Italians are tempted to applaud more of those performances which stray dangerously farthest from reality, those which make do with the scantiest of materials, those which do not even pretend to imitate existing models and still manage to be effective, convincing, stirring or entertaining. Take imitation marble. Since the earliest days local craftsmen have been unique in their ability to counterfeit the real thing. Half the marble one sees in churches or patrician palazzi is in fact but smooth plaster deceptively painted.
—Barzini 1968, 111

Figure 76
Fake carbon fiber
ebay.com

Figure 77
Fake checker plate
bunnings.com.au

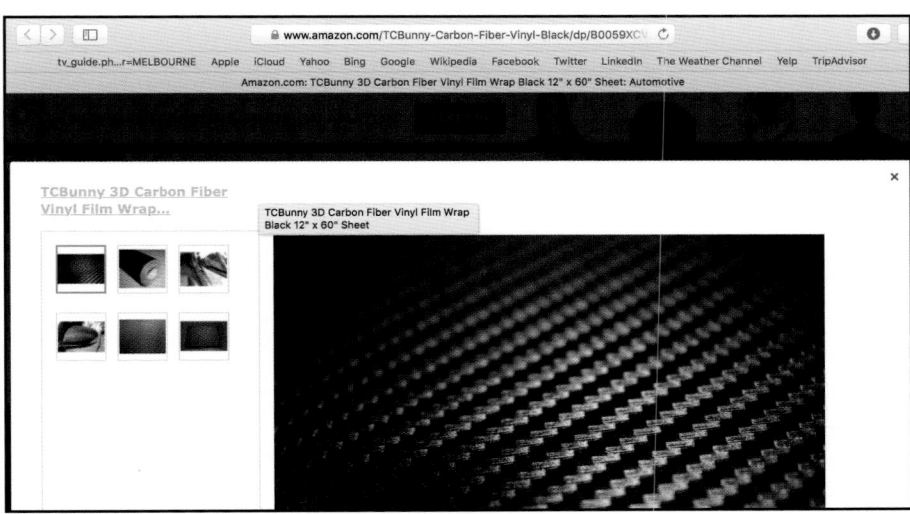

76

77

Substitution
Who cares?

We all need care in some parts of our life. Childhood, periods of illness, and old age each have their needs. But some of us also have the need to give care— parents, of course, but also pet owners and many others, among them people who themselves need care. Children give care to teddy bears, dolls, and pets. Hospital inpatients and residents in nursing homes sometimes feel a similar need. To meet this need is part of the mission of mental commitment robots. Animal-assisted therapy (by live animals) is therapy aimed at improving patients' social, emotional, and cognitive functioning. Therapy involving live animals, however, may involve problems which Paro the mental commitment robot doesn't (Shibata 2012). Among these avoided problems are cultural barriers, diseases passed on from animal to human, and insect infestation.

Paro is a robot baby seal that provides the closeness and comfort that people suffering from dementia and other illnesses may miss more than anything else. Paro does no physical work, but provides mental services. It allegedly functions psychologically, physiologically, and socially. Paro inspires people to undertake mental and physical activity, and provides something for them to talk about. Paro emulates a baby seal by appearance, the sensation of touch, and autonomous behavior. Paro perceives its environment, including the interacting human, through several sensors that address touch, light, sound, temperature, and posture. It reacts by making sounds and moving its head and legs. It reacts to its given name and remembers and repeats preferred behavior. In 2009, the US Food and Drug Administration (FDA) certified Paro as a biofeedback medical device.

Figure 78
Paro, the mental commitment robot
Design: Takanori Shibata, 1993
Manufacturer: AIST, Japan
Length: 55 cm; weight: 2.7 kg

78

Substitution
Who cares?

Pleo is a toy dinosaur modeled after a baby camarasaurus that lived in North America 145 to 155 million years ago. Pleo learns from its experiences and develops from puppy to adolescent to a grown-up with a "personality." It also emits dinosaur-like sounds. Pleo has soft polymeric skin that wears depending on how it is treated. A number of sensors allow Pleo to react to touch and sounds. When its back is touched, Pleo turns its head as if to see who did it. It also turns its head when it is talked to.

79

Figure 79
Pleo
Design: Caleb Chung, 2006
Manufacturer: Innvo Labs Corporation, United States
Length: 53 cm; weight: 4.0 kg

Substitution
Placeholders

Physical models and mock-ups are abstractions of the real things, proxies used for practical and economical reasons. Some physical models mimic the original as much as possible, while others just abstract relevant characteristics. The fashion designer's and window dresser's mannequins, the shoemaker's lasts, and the hat maker's wooden skulls—all placeholders for prospective customers—belong to the latter category. Ex ante models predate something to come, while ex post models record what has been. Models, like other substitutes, denote the substituted; if not the whole thing, then at least certain features relevant for use. Connotation hardly plays any role. Wooden legs with the connotation of pirate belong to the past.

Gliedermann models are articulated imitations of the human skeleton or selected parts, typically hands and feet, which provide students and artists with in-depth understanding of the human construction. Anatomical models of the eye, nose, and ear are typically larger than life, while architectural models, with prominent exceptions, are smaller. Taxidermy animals have a natural size, and can serve as study material as well as hunting trophies.

When Mies van der Rohe designed a villa in The Hague in 1912 for Dutch art collectors Helene and Anton Kröller, he built a four-meter-tall mock-up of wood and canvas in the actual setting (Schulze 1985, 63). In spite of, or perhaps because of, this effort, the real house was not commissioned. Before kicking off the building of La Grande Arche in Paris, President François Mitterrand had the largest mobile crane in France elevate a building component to the planned height in La Défense to check the visual impact (Radosavljevic and Bennett 2012, 41).

Flight simulators let pilots safely train for dangerous situations which they hope they will never experience in real life, such as landing without running motors or with the breakdown of electric or hydraulic systems. Marine simulators let ship builders and ship officers learn in cost-effective ways the properties of large vessels—for example, how to navigate a supertanker in narrow conditions.

LEGO Architecture comprises sets of toy bricks that when assembled make models of famous edifices: Villa Savoye, the Flatiron Building, Rockefeller Center, the leaning tower of Pisa, and many more.

**Figure 80
Gliedermann,
wooden mannequin
artist's model**

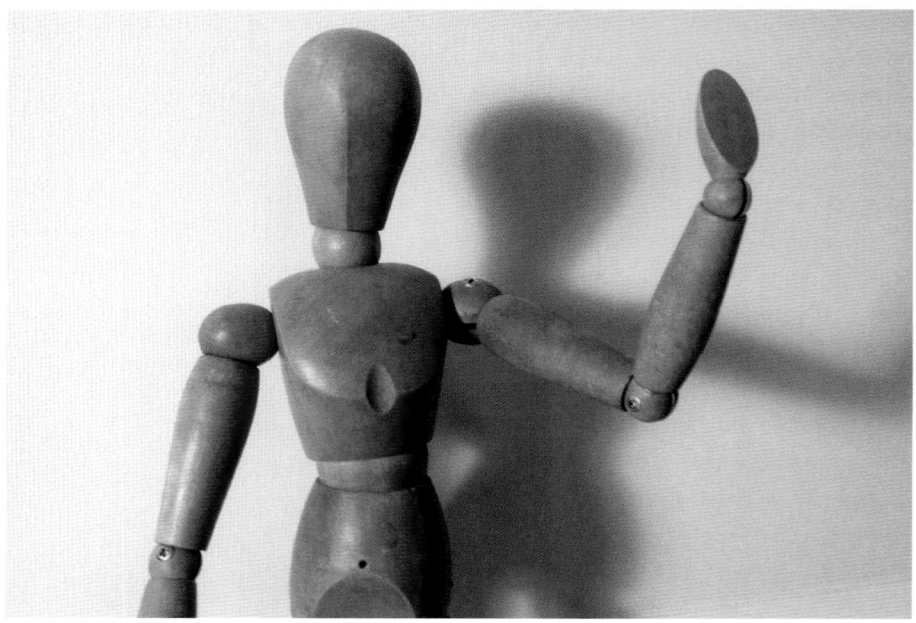

80

81

Figure 81
Japanese display
dishes in restaurant
window

82

**Figure 82
LEGO Architecture,
Rockefeller Center
Manufacturer: LEGO,
Denmark**

**Figure 83
Doctor's lady, ivory**
Chinese doctors'
female clients would
point at the figure
instead of their own
body to show the
location of their
physical ailment.

**Figure 84
Mounted kangaroo**
Taxidermy gives
animals a second life
as study material or
trophies.

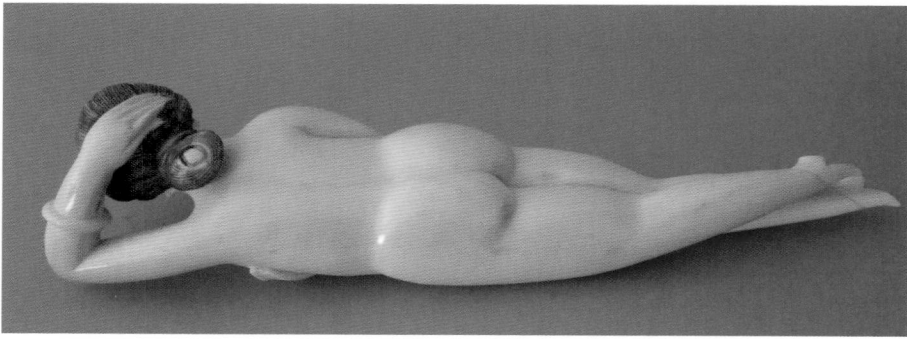

83

84

Deception

All warfare is based on deception.
—Sun Tzu (544–496 BCE)

Mundus vult decipi, ergo decipiatur.
The world wants to be deceived, so let it be deceived.
—Several attributions

Deception
The truth suspended

Pretense design bends the truth. Our categories of pretense objectives—beautification, amusement, and depending on the intention, substitution—include innocent types of pretense design, where the truth most often is edited or on standby. The addressees are beneficiaries rather than victims of the pretense. The fourth objective category, deception, deals with pretense design where the truth is suspended. Now we are talking about cheating.

In the deception branch of pretense design, the addressee is an opponent in an existing or possible conflict. The pretender misguides the addressees (alias opponents) by counterfactual information about the true state of affairs. The addressees are deceived at their own disadvantage. Hard-core material deception takes place in several fields including warfare, hunting, fishing, and gardening, as well as several varieties of plagiarism and other infringement of intellectual property rights.

The martial use of pretense design notably includes hiding by camouflage, but also simulation of a threatening presence created to fool the enemy. The latter method is also applied by gardeners whose scarecrows keep fruit-eating birds away.

Hunters and fishermen use decoys and spoon bait respectively to tempt and attract their prey. Hunters, bird watchers, and animal photographers use camouflage to pass unseen.

Disguising himself to achieve advantages wrongfully was the case when the proverbial Captain from Köpenick, an out-of-work Prussian disguised in a stolen military uniform, emptied his town's cashbox (see p. 28). Webpages that pretend to be "official" but are false intruders constitute a new but already numerous category.

85

Figure 85
Scarecrow
The scarecrow's function is similar to that of much military camouflage: discouraging unwanted visitors.

Bank robbers and aggressive protesters at political summit meetings stereotypically use balaclavas or hoods with eyeholes to remain incognito to staff, surveillance cameras, and police when committing their offense. Hangmen also used to hide their face, and so do Ku Klux Klansmen.

Deceitful packaging that contains less of a product than indicated by appearance is found in many places, especially containers for chocolate, cosmetics, and computer software. Are buyers of these products especially naïve, or do they have short memories? These packaging tricks must be classified as deception. A special kind of deceitful packaging happens when a company invisibly reduces the content of a package without reducing the price accordingly. The trick is that a hardly noticeable 10% reduction of the content means a hidden 11% increase of the price. If the product's price had been increased openly, buyers might have refrained from buying. There are limits to how many times the contents can be reduced without offering an empty package. Before this situation is reached, the company may resize the quantity to the original magnitude, advertise the increase, and raise the price accordingly. Foxed buyers may find this OK because the quantity has visibly increased. That done, the company can start reducing the contents in invisible steps again. Sellers don't necessarily find this iterative strategy deceitful because the quantity is stated on the package, allowing observant buyers to see what they get: *caveat emptor,* buyer beware.

Denoting the false as if it were true is the true nature of deception.

Deception
The truth suspended

Unauthorized copying, infringement of intellectual property right, is a theft of thoughts, or rather theft of the use of thoughts. Forgery, as known in the art world, may also take place in the world of design. It involves the wholesale production of fraudulent imitation objects. Design copying is copious and keeps armies of lawyers busy all over the world.

Whether deceptive design is a wrongdoing depends on several factors, including vantage point, morals, and law. To mislead the enemy in war and to fool animals when hunting and fishing are acceptable, as seen from the deceivers' point of view. Misleading fellow beings to achieve economic gain is immoral, and possibly in conflict with the law. Deception, as defined here, always means suspending the truth.

Figure 86
Vendetta masks marketed by Amazon
This Guy Fawkes mask is based on one designed by David Lloyd for *V for Vendetta,* a graphic novel (Moore 1982). Amazon's annual sales of Guy Fawkes masks allegedly surpass the hundreds of thousands ("Guy," En.wikipedia.org **2017).**

Sponsored ⓘ
V wie for Vendetta Mask - Guy Fawkes Mask - Beige Halloween Karneval Anonymous
by Goods & Gadgets

EUR 7.95 **EUR 2.95** + EUR 2.95 delivery ☆☆☆☆☆ ▾ 4

2015 NEW V wie Vendetta Maske mit Eyeliner Nostril Anonymous Guy Fawkes Fancy Adult Kostüm Zubehör Halloween-Maske Boolavard Ltd
by V MASK

EUR 7.70 ✓*Prime*
Get it by Tuesday, Dec 20

More buying choices
EUR 2.49 new (2 offers)
EUR 5.38 used (2 offers)

☆☆☆☆☆ ▾ 7
Eligible for FREE Delivery.
Manufacturer recommended age: 12 - 50 Years
Toys & Games: See all 385 items

Boolavard ® TM V für Vendetta Guy Fawkes Anonymous Die Maske Halloween Masken Cosplay VENDETTA Maske Mask Guy Fawkes Anonymous Replika Demo Anti -Karneval Maske Anti Acta...
by Boolavard® TM

EUR 0.99 + EUR 5.39 delivery ☆☆☆☆☆ ▾ 3
Toys & Games: See all 385 items

86

Deception
Masks

Masks are tools for protection, hiding, and pretense.
While hiding and pretense may aim at deception,
protection falls outside the subject of this section.
Masks for protection may protect the wearer as well
as those around the wearer. Welders wear masks to
protect themselves, doctors wear them to protect
themselves and their patients.

The simplest masks for hiding have anonymous
fronts, such as those used by protesters, bank
robbers, and police on special missions. Such masks
are typically balaclavas or hoods with holes for eyes,
and perhaps for the mouth. Sometimes a paper
shopping bag with holes for the eyes serves a similar
function.

When masks are used for serious deception,
the focus is on hiding the truth, hiding the true
identity of someone. "Anonymous"[1] members with
Guy Fawkes masks have one leg in both camps. They
want to protect themselves by hiding who they are
as individuals, but at the same time they want to
advertise their menace as a highly profiled group. Ku
Klux Klan cones also protect the wearers' identity
while promoting their hateful organization.

When police officers occasionally hide their
individuality behind balaclavas, they as a rule openly
show their group affiliation by their uniform or
prescribed combat dress. Witnesses sometimes wear
masks to hide their identity at trials. Hijabs and burqas
are veils and enveloping outer garments, respectively,
worn by Muslim women for religious reasons.

Masks for carnival and theater constitute the
amusement branch of face covering (see p. 29). When
for pleasure, the focus may be on showing the false,
showing something that is not true, or just hiding.

[1] Anonymous is an
informally organized
group of activists
and hacktivists who
have adopted the Guy
Fawkes mask.

Deception
Cartography

Geographical maps constitute a special province of pretense design. They never tell the truth, the whole truth, and nothing but the truth. Maps always include elements of distortion. The perfect geographical map does not exist.

Geographical maps are abstractions. First, they are planar descriptions of spherical realities. Flat, two-dimensional maps describing a three-dimensional world can never be more than approximate. Second, maps are always in small scale; they are smaller than the reality they depict. Third, maps use symbols to describe real-world phenomena, and these symbols are proportionally oversized. If a road were shown on the map in the proportionally correct thickness, it would be invisible to the human eye. Fourth, maps are always edited. The cartographer has chosen what to show and—equally important—what to omit.

The above four types of map "errors" are *bona fide* necessary evils, indispensable parts of the game. Other map errors are *mala fide,* done deliberately to deceive the users. Political rulers, sales people, and developers may find it expedient to commission maps that are tendentious and distort facts.

A nation that aspires to acquire more *Lebensraum* may prematurely include their territorial claims in official maps and maybe appropriate the desired territory verbally by giving it a new name. Maps showing territorial claims may be disseminated as motifs on postage stamps.

Figures 87, 88
Postage stamps are a handy medium for airing territorial claims.

Figure 87
Argentine postage stamp, 1951
The stamp presents Argentina's Antarctic territorial claim, the area between the 24°W and the 74°W meridians, as a reality. However, the British claim, 20°W–80°W, and the Chilean claim, 54°W–90°W, overlap Argentina's claim. All claims were suspended by the Antarctic Treaty System that regulates the area between 60°S and the South Pole.

Figure 88
Argentine postage stamp, 1976
The stamp features the (British) Falkland Islands (Islas Malvinas in Spanish). Argentina issued stamps featuring the Falkland Islands both before and after the Falkland War in 1982.

87

88

Sales people and developers may distort sizes, omit unwanted noisy and otherwise polluting elements, and exaggerate desired elements such as closeness to natural attractions or public transport facilities.

Publishers of maps sometimes include copyright traps—small errors such as the inclusion of a nonexistent road, "trap street," or a fictitious bend in a road. If a competitor wrongfully copies the map, copyright traps may prove useful in a court case. In 2001 the British Automobile Association paid 20 million pounds in an out-of-court settlement to the British Ordnance Survey after having plagiarized their maps, including copyright traps (Clark 2001). Copyright traps—fabricated geographical features or names—are one kind of pretense design used to prevent another kind of pretense design. One of Churchill's quips comes to mind: "In wartime, truth is so precious that she should always be attended by a bodyguard of lies."

Phantom islands, or nonexistent islands, are seen on early maps, e.g. on *Theatrum Orbis Terrarum* (1574) by Abraham Ortelius, the world's first atlas. The North Atlantic Sea is adorned with three nonexistent islands: Brazil, Frieslandt, and Grocklandt. Today, map designers occasionally burnish their reputations by lending their own name to a mountain or other geographical feature. Maps are always distortions, and sometimes include deliberate lies.

89

**Figure 89
The world's first
atlas, *Theatrum
Orbis Terrarum,*
Abraham Ortelius
1574**
The map of the
North Atlantic Sea
includes three
phantom islands:
Brazil, Frieslandt, and
Grocklandt. Attitudes
toward cartographic
precision have
changed since the
sixteenth century.

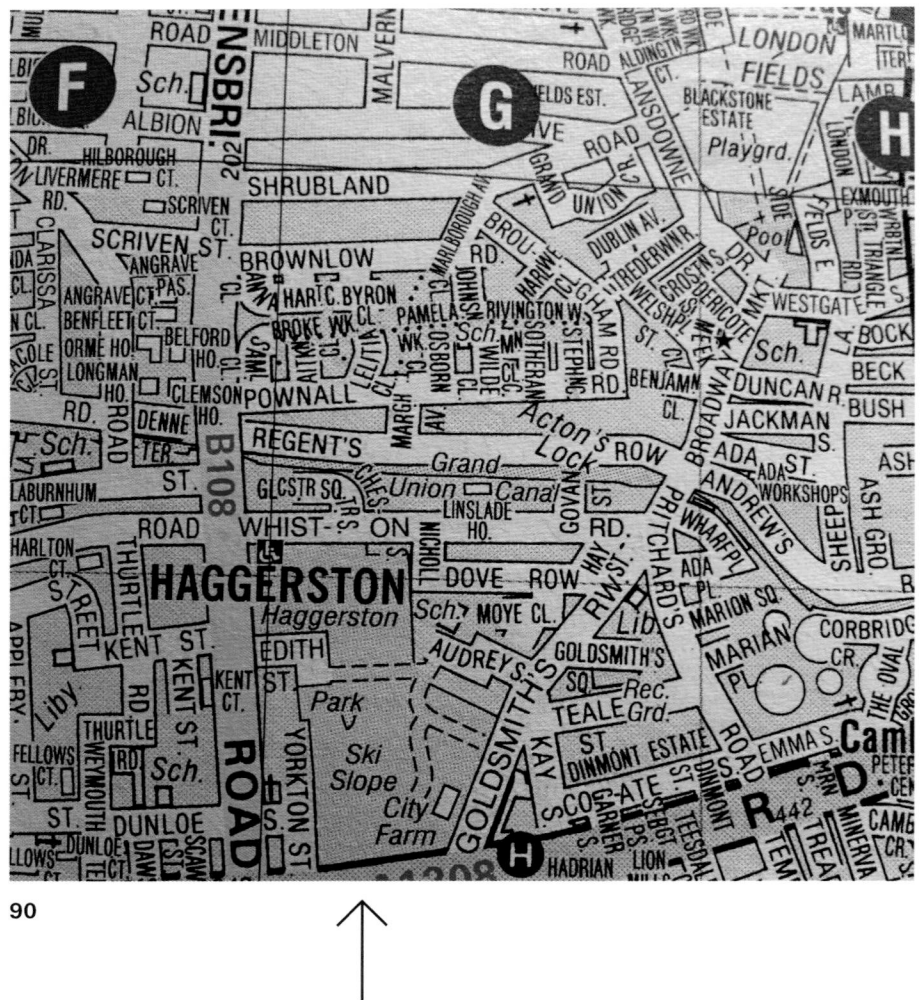

90

Figure 90
London A-Z
Ski Slope Haggerston
is a copy trap
detected, and then
removed in later
issues (Jacobs 2017).

Deception
Trojan horses

The Trojan horse described in Homer's *Odyssey* and in Virgil's *Aeneid* played a decisive role in the Greek siege of Troy, an ancient city in present-day northwestern Anatolia in Turkey. After having given up the siege, the Greeks left a large wooden horse on wheels as a gift of peace. When the Trojans took the horse inside, a door in the horse opened and out came a large number of soldiers who then opened the gates of Troy to let in the Greek army. The Trojan horse is fiction, and we don't know the exact position of Troy, but the concept lives on.

In the world of computer hacks, a Trojan horse is malware, malicious software. An apparently harmless program hides its harmful content until it is loaded on the victim's computer. Then it wreaks havoc on the computer's contents.

91

**Figure 91
The Trojan horse
from *Vatican Virgil*,
a manuscript with
fragments of Virgil's
*Aeneid***

Deception
Potemkin village

The term "Potemkin village" stands for façades
that significantly oversell what is behind them. The
expression is widely used metaphorically. It owes its
eponym to Russian minister Grigori Aleksandrovich
Potemkin, who reportedly built fake settlements
along the river Dnieper to impress Empress Catherine
II during her 1787 visit to Crimea. He wanted the
conquered land to appear extra valuable to the
inspecting empress and her entourage ("Potemkin,"
En.wikipedia.org 2017).

Before Hitler's visit to Rome in 1938,
Mussolini, following Potemkin's example, revamped
all house fronts along the railway line from Brenner at
the Austrian border to Rome (Barzini 1968, 176). The
eternal city also got a treat, described by the Italian
dialect poet Trilussa, here in translation (Barzini 1968,
101):

> Rome of travertine,
> re-made with cardboard,
> greets the house painter,
> who will be her next master.

Hitler had his own Potemkin village. The
concentration camp Theresienstadt was designed
to appear as a model camp to be presented to
the Red Cross and used in propaganda movies.
Theresienstadt was in reality a genuine KZ camp,
where a fourth of the 140,000 prisoners died from
illness and almost 90,000 were sent to Auschwitz for
execution ("Theresienstadt," En.wikipedia.org 2017).

Contemporary Potemkin-like manifestations
would include the sometimes superficial ways cities
dress up for political visits, international summits,
and Olympic Games.

Figure 92
Theresienstadt,
concentration camp
Theresienstadt was
a Potemkin village in
the worst sense of
that term.

Figure 93
Kijong-dong, North
Korea
An empty village in
the demilitarized zone
between North and
South Korea, built to
impress the latter.

92

93

Deception
Camouflage

Camouflage has been inspired by nature, developed by artists and scientists, and primarily used by the military. The word "camouflage" originates from *camouflet*, French for "cloud of smoke," and its related meaning "to blow smoke into someone's face." Camouflage hides or blurs existence and identity. French camoufleurs developed military camouflage during World War I, with the objective of protecting soldiers from observation by enemy forces. However, a balance must always be sought between hiding and distinguishing friend from foe.

Animals have inspired the human use of camouflage. Predators practice aggressive camouflage to approach their prey unseen. Prey use defensive camouflage to remain unseen, or to disinterest or scare away predators. Both aggressive and defensive camouflage can work by general resemblance or special resemblance.

General resemblance means similarity to the background, which implies that different geographical areas and different seasons demand different camouflage. Some species with coats of fur or feathers that make it difficult to discern them from their background change appearance with the season. For example, the polar fox has white fur in winter and brown fur in summer. The chameleon changes color with short notice to match its background, and possibly also according to its mood.

General resemblance may be reinforced by disruptive coloring, or disturbing color patterns, which makes it difficult for predators to discern the outlines of an animal. The same effect makes it difficult to distinguish the single animal in the pack. Zebras have disruptive coloring.

94

95

Figure 94
Prickly insect, native to New Zealand
Defensive camouflage with special resemblance

Figure 95
Owl butterfly
Is the eyespot pattern on the wings of the owl butterfly an example of defensive mimicry that scares possible predators? Some naturalists think so.

Special resemblance, or mimicry, involves hiding by looking like other organisms, whether animal or vegetable. The plant-hopper insect looks like a leaf, which may disinterest birds looking for a meat dish. The prickly stick insect looks like a part of the plant it lives on. The owl butterfly has a wing image that justifies its name.

Animals inspired the military use of camouflage when new martial technology made it necessary. Camouflage of personnel was introduced, as an answer to the introduction of long-range firearms, while later camouflage of equipment and installations on the ground was an answer to aerial reconnaissance. Military forces, like animals, use camouflage for defense and aggression. They most often hide by general resemblance, often reinforced by disruptive coloring.

Before the emergence of long-range firearms, armies would dress in conspicuous colors intended to make it easy to distinguish between friend and foe and, probably, to boost the *esprit de corps*. The ongoing material dialogue between armies, where each army reacts to the counterpart's technology for hitting and hiding, changed this.

In the eighteenth century, Austrian *Grenzers* (border soldiers) and *Jägers* (hunters) with green jackets inspired Prussian king Frederick the Great to establish his own battalion with green jackets. Later, England introduced rifle green uniforms. In India, England developed khaki uniforms, but that was primarily for climatic reasons rather than for camouflage. Nevertheless the idea spread.

Deception
Camouflage

96

97

Figure 96
Wallaby
The wallaby practices
defensive camouflage
by general
resemblance to its
natural surroundings.

Figure 97
US Hospital
Corpsman, 3rd
Marine Regiment,
in the vicinity
of Mehtar Lam,
Afghanistan, 2005

Deception
Camouflage

During World War I, German, British, and
American troops fought in plain gray or green
uniforms that did not stand out too much in the
landscape. French troops entered the war with blue
jackets and red trousers, but took an object lesson
and changed to less conspicuous, discreet horizon-
blue uniforms.

Camouflage uniforms with printed patterns
were first introduced in World War II. In the
campaign in Russia, Germany used a camouflage
pattern, *Zeltbahn*, in a double-sided version: white for
winter, brown for summer—reminiscent of the polar
fox. British and American use of printed camouflage
uniforms in World War II was only marginal.
However, the United States used camouflage combat
uniforms in combat against Japan in the Pacific
and later at the landing in Normandy. Patterned
camouflage was, however, abandoned due to the
resemblance to the German combat uniform.

After World War II, the United States
developed camouflage uniforms with printed patterns
for the Vietnam War and later the Gulf War, the war
in Iraq, and the engagement in Afghanistan. Today,
most nations seem to develop their own camouflage
pattern for combat uniforms.

Camouflage of vehicles, weapons, ships, and
aircraft was introduced in World War I when aerial
reconnaissance became a reality. Much attention
was given to disruptive coloring, or "dazzle," as it was
called in England. Germany, France, England, and
the United States all called upon artists for expertise.
Blurring outlines by stark contrasts between bright
and dark proved more important than specific colors.
Picasso and others have pointed at a connection
between camouflage and cubism.

Figure 98
US Army testing
Future Force Warrior
components, 2007
Defensive/aggressive
camouflage, general
resemblance

Figure 99
Arthur Lismer:
RMS *Olympic*
(dazzle painted) with
Returned Soldiers
in Halifax after
WWI
Defensive
camouflage,
disruptive coloring

98, 99

Deception
Camouflage

Today camouflage patterns inspired by simple observation of nature and designed by artists have given way to digital camouflage, scientifically based patterns that provide camouflage over a range of distances. Also, modern camouflage of personnel and equipment addresses night-vision technology and other advanced detection methods.

Stealth aircraft are designed with special concern for camouflage, and there is more than meets the eye. Shape and surface are designed to defy radar and other types of advanced detection. New ways of detecting stealth effects, and new ways to avoid these, will keep the defense industry busy for years to come.

**Figure 100
Nighthawk Stealth Fighter, 2002, United States**
Stealth airplanes with faceted surfaces have a low radar signature and also defy other detection methods. Defensive/aggressive camouflage, general resemblance.

**Figure 101
The corvette HMS *Visby* in the harbor of Visby, Sweden**
Traditional visual camouflage is combined with anti-radar stealth design. Defensive/aggressive camouflage, general resemblance.

100

101

Birdwatchers, hunters, and others who want
to pass unnoticed in nature may be interested in
Cabela's ColorPhase technology (Cabela 2017).
Perhaps inspired by the polar fox's color shift
between winter and summer, this invention lets
camouflage clothing printed with rapid-change,
temperature-activated dye change with the
temperature. When the temperatures are high in
spring and summer, the clothing will be greenish.
When the temperatures drop in autumn, the clothing
will turn brownish.

Fishing lures and flies are manmade bait
that attract fish by their similarity to prey, in color,
vibration, and movement. Lures may look like fish;
flies may look like fish, crustaceans, or insects. Web
designers design "link bait" and "click bait," material
on a website that attracts visitors.

102

**Figure 102
Heddon lure for
salmon fishing**
Aggressive
camouflage, special
resemblance.

**Figure 103
Decoys: duck,
goose, and swan**
Aggressive
camouflage, special
resemblance.

103

The distinction between laudable learning from others and plagiarism is not always totally clear, but is important. The evolution of society builds on learning from each other. Buckminster Fuller (1969, 278) used the phrase "continuous man" to refer to our ability to learn from, and work together with, others in the past and present. Scientists stand on the shoulders of each other and, as a rule, acknowledge this. Designers also meticulously study the past and present, and build on the work by their predecessors, distant or close. They do so with different intentions and different results. Some take inspiration; others cite, emulate, or copy. There are no sharp demarcation lines between these past-praising activities.

Kaare Klint, the father of modern Danish furniture design, taught his students at the Royal Danish Academy in Copenhagen to study the past carefully. Studying existing furniture design was the best point of departure for designing new furniture. Of course something should be improved, added, or subtracted. Klint blazed the trail. He simplified his sources of inspiration—for example, the Chippendale chair that inspired his famous Red Chair (Mollerup 2015).

Plagiarism is sometimes euphemized as sincere flattery; originality is occasionally, tongue-in-cheek, defined as undiscovered plagiarism. Both statements tend to whitewash plagiarism. The often-repeated adage "Amateurs imitate, artists steal" was possibly inspired by T. S. Eliot (1920): "Immature poets imitate; mature poets steal; bad poets deface what they take, and good poets make it into something better, or at least something different."

None of these quips changes the fact that serious plagiarism is serious theft. The stolen item is not an original idea, and it is still there. The theft is the use of the original idea. Manufacturers of copies of famous furniture by the Eameses and many others constitute a sad group of design-based commerce. Their chosen route from an existing to a preferred situation is dishonest. Shame on manufacturers and sellers alike—as well as their buyers.

Postscript

Design is an agent of change, change for the better, change for preferred situations, as phrased by Nobel Laureate Herbert Simon (1996, 111). Pretense design is an expedited route from existing to preferred situations.

Bona fide pretense design results in happiness, entertainment, reduced pain, savings, and other preferred effects. *Mala fide* pretense design presents a disadvantage for the addressees. This fact, however, should not mean we say goodbye to all pretense design, just as we don't blacklist kitchen utensils because they occasionally are used for domestic violence.

Without pretense design, people would look less attractive, people with a missing limb would suffer from reduced functionality and perhaps stigmatization, theaters would be dull, and we would compromise our health by eating more butter (some dietitians may challenge this argument). Furniture would be less durable and more expensive, and so on. Good designers know the grammar of *bona fide* pretense design. Teachers, writers, and design thinkers should update their thinking by learning from design practice, which—as usual—runs ahead of design theory. Pretense design—with some deplorable exceptions—improves quality of life.

Bibliography

Augustine. (2017). "On Lying" (De mendacio). http://www.newadvent.org/
     fathers/1312.htm (accessed 16 September).

Bacon, F. (1909/1914). *Essays, Civil and Moral*. Cambridge: Harvard Classics.

Barzini, L. (1968). *The Italians*. New York: Simon & Schuster.

Baudrillard, J. (1968/1996). *The System of Objects*. London: Verso.

Bell, J., and B. Whaley. (1991). *Cheating and Deception*. New Brunswick, NJ:
     Transaction Publishers.

Benjamin, W. (2010). *The Work of Art in the Age of Mechanical Reproduction*.
     Lexington, KY: Prism Key Press.

Bosker, B. (2013). *Original Copies*. Honolulu: University of Hawai'i Press.

Bricker, T. (2017). "Here You Leave Today and Enter the World of Yesterday,
     Tomorrow and Fantasy." Disney tourist blog. http://www.
     disneytouristblog. com/here-you-leave-today-and-enter-the-world-of-
     yesterday-tomorrow-and-fantasy/ (accessed 20 October).

Brown, J. (2007). *The Self.* New York: Routledge.

Buchannan, R. (1985). "Declaration by Design: Rhetoric, Argument, and
     Demonstration in Design Practice." *Design Issues* 2(1): 4.

Buildingpharmabrands. (2013). "Does She .... or Doesn't She?" Available
     at: https://buildingpharmabrands.com/2013/04/08/does-she-or-
     doesnt-she/ (accessed 12 October 2017).

Burroughs, A. (2007). *Everyday Engineering*. San Francisco: Chronicle Books.

Cabela. (2017). "Cabela's ColorPhase Camo—Color Changing Camouflage."
     https://www.cabelas.com/category/Cabelas-ColorPhase/396159480.uts
     (accessed 15 October 2017).

Cancerinstitute.org.au. (2018). "Dark Side of Tanning campaign." Cancer
     Institute NSW. Available at: https://www.cancerinstitute.org.au/how-we-
     help/cancer-prevention/skin-cancer-prevention/campaigns/dark-side-of-
     tanning-campaign (accessed 9 January 2018).

Charney, N. (2014). *The Art of Forgery*. London: Phaidon Press.

Clark, A. (2017). "Copying Maps Costs AA £20m." *Guardian*, 6 March. Available
     at: https://www.theguardian.com/uk/2001/mar/06/andrewclark (accessed
     14 October 2017).

Danmarkshistorien.dk. (2017). "MYTE: Var Christian 10.s hest ved Genforeningen
     kalket hvid?" Available at: http://danmarkshistorien.dk/leksikon-og-
     kilder/vis/materiale/myte-var-christian-10s-hest-ved-genforeningen-
     kalket-hvid/ (accessed 14 September 2017).

DePaolo, B. (2010). *The Hows and Whys of Lies*. Lexington, KY: CreateSpace
     Independent Publishing Platform.

De.wikipedia.org. (2017). "Schmiss." Available at: https://de.wikipedia.org/wiki/
     Schmiss (accessed 20 October 2017).

Durrell, L. (1958). *Balthazar*. London: Faber and Faber.

Eco, U. (1972). "Towards a Semiotic Inquiry into the Television Message." *Working Papers in Cultural Studies* 3:103-121.

--- (1986). *Travels in Superreality*. Fort Washington, PA: Harvest Books.

--- (1997). *A Theory of Semiotics*. Bloomington: Indiana University Press.

Economist.com. (2014). "The Bilbao Effect." In "Temples of Delight," special issue of *The Economist*, January 6. Available at: https://www.economist.com/news/special-report/21591708-if-you-build-it-will-they-come-bilbao-effect (accessed 14 September 2017).

Edmonds, M. (2011). "How Makeup Works." HowStuffWorks. http://people.howstuffworks.com/about-makeup1.htm (accessed 6 October 2017).

Encyclopedia Britannica. (2017). "Trojan Horse | Greek Mythology." Available at: https://www.britannica.com/topic/Trojan-horse (accessed 14 October 2017).

En.wikipedia.org. (2017). "Boat Shoe." Available at: https://en.wikipedia.org/wiki/Boat_shoe (accessed 6 October 2017).

--- (2017). "Demi's Birthday Suit." Available at: https://en.wikipedia.org/wiki/Demi%27s_Birthday_Suit (accessed 17 September 2017).

--- (2017). "Facadism." Available at: https://en.wikipedia.org/wiki/Facadism (accessed 13 October 2017).

--- (2017). "Forced Perspective." Available at: https://en.wikipedia.org/wiki/Forced_perspective (accessed 13 October 2017).

--- (2017). "Guy Fawkes Mask." Available at: https://en.wikipedia.org/wiki/Guy_Fawkes_mask (accessed 16 September 2017).

--- (2017). "High-Heeled Footwear." Available at: https://en.wikipedia.org/wiki/High-heeled_shoefootwear (accessed 6 October 2017).

--- (2017). "Irezumi." Available at: https://en.wikipedia.org/wiki/Irezumi (accessed 21 October 2017).

--- (2017). "L'Oréal." Available at: https://en.wikipedia.org/wiki/L'%27Oréal (accessed 9 October 2017).

--- (2017). "Paul A. Sperry." Available at: https://en.wikipedia.org/wiki/Paul_A._Sperry (accessed 12 October 2017).

--- (2017). "Potemkin Village." Available at: https://en.wikipedia.org/wiki/Potemkin_village (accessed 16 October 2017).

--- (2017). "Prussian Army." Available at: https://en.wikipedia.org/wiki/Prussian_Army (accessed 9 October 2017).

--- (2017). "Shabby Chic." Available at: https://en.wikipedia.org/wiki/Shabby_chic (accessed 20 October 2017).

--- (2018). "Skopje 2014." Available at: https://en.wikipedia.org/wiki/Skopje_2014 (accessed 27 February 2018).

--- (2017). "Steampunk." Available at: https://en.wikipedia.org/wiki/Steampunk (accessed 20 October 2017).

--- (2017). "Sun Tanning." Available at: https://en.wikipedia.org/
wiki/Sun_tanning (accessed 4 October 2017).

--- (2017). "Theresienstadt Concentration Camp." Available at:
https://en.wikipedia.org/wiki/Theresienstadt_concentration_
camp#Statistics (accessed 20 October 2017).

--- (2017). "Warsaw Old Town." Available at: https://en.wikipedia.org/wiki/
Warsaw_Old_Town (accessed 13 October 2017).

--- (2017). "Wilhelm Voigt." Available at: https:/en.wikipedia.
org/wiki/Wilhelm_Voigt (accessed 16 September 2017).

Fuller, B. (1969). *Ideas and Integrities: A Spontaneous Autobiographical
Disclosure.* New York: Prentice-Hall.

Giedion, S. (1948). *Mechanization Takes Command: A Contribution to
Anonymous History.* New York: Oxford University Press.

Goffman, E. (1959). *The Presentation of Self in Everyday Life.* New York: Anchor
Books.

Grayling, A. (2010). *Thinking of Answers.* New York: Walker Publishing.

Gros, J. (1987). *Grundlagen einer Theorie der Produktsprache.* Offenbach am
Main: Hochschule für Gestaltung, Fachbereich Produktgestaltung.

Hofstadter, D., and E. Sander. (2013). *Surfaces and Essences: Analogy as the
Fuel and Fire of Thinking.* New York: Basic Books.

IKEA. (1993). *Svenskt 1700-tal på IKEA.* Inter IKEA Systems.

IMDb. (2017). *Casablanca* (1942). Available at: http://www.imdb.com/title/t
0034583/trivia (accessed 6 October 2017).

Jacobs, F. (2017). "Help Find London's Missing Map Traps!" Big Think. Available
at: http://bigthink.com/strange-maps/where-are-londons-missing-map-
traps (accessed 19 September 2017).

Lauren, R. (2007). *Ralph Lauren.* New York: Rizzoli.

Le Corbusier. (1923). *Towards a New Architecture.* monoskop.org/images/b/bf/
Corbusier_Le_Towards_a_New_Architecture_no_OCR.pdf (accessed 20
October 2017).

Lewin, S. (1991). *Formica and Design.* New York: Rizzoli.

McCracken, G. (1990). *Culture and Consumption.* Bloomington: Indiana
University Press.

Miodownik, M. (2014). *Stuff Matters: The Strange Stories of the Marvellous
Materials That Shape Our Man-Made World.* London: Penguin.

Mollerup, P. (2015). *Simplicity: A Matter of Design.* Amsterdam: BIS Publishers.
monoskop.org/images/b/bf/Corbusier_Le_Towards_a_New_Architecture_
no_OCR.pdf (accessed 20 October2017).

Moore, A. (1982). *V for Vendetta.* Marblehead, MA: Vertigo.

Panofsky, E., W. Heckscher, and I. Lavin. (1997). *Three Essays on Style.*
Cambridge, MA: MIT Press.

Radosavljevic, M., and J. Bennett. (2012). *Construction Management Strategies:*

A Theory of Construction Management. New York: John Wiley & Sons.

Robinson, K. (2011). *Out of Our Minds.* Chichester, UK: Capstone Publishing.

Rudofsky, B. (1984). *The Unfashionable Human Body.* New York: Van Nostrand Reinhold.

Ruskin, J. (1880). *The Stones of Venice.* New York: John Wiley.

Schulze, F. (1985). *Mies van der Rohe: A Critical Biography.* Chicago: University of Chicago Press.

Shibata, T. (2012). "Therapeutic Seal Robot as Biofeedback Medical Device: Qualitative and Quantitative Evaluations of Robot Therapy in Dementia Care." *IEEE* 100(8) (August): 2527–2538.

Simon, H. (1996). *The Sciences of the Artificial.* Cambridge, MA: MIT Press.

Spivack, E. (2012). "Paint-on Hosiery During the War Years." Smithsonian. September 10. https://www.smithsonianmag.com/arts-culture/paint-on-hosiery-during-the-war-years-29864389/ (accessed 4 October 2017).

"Story of Cities #28: How Postwar Warsaw Was Rebuilt Using 18th Century Paintings." (2016). *The Guardian,* April 22. https://www.theguardian.com/cities/2016/apr/22/story-cities-warsaw-rebuilt-18th-century-paintings (accessed 25 October 2017)

Tall Men Shoes. (2017). "Height Increasing Elevator Shoes for Man's Tall." Tallmenshoes.com (accessed 20 October)

Thefullwiki.org. (2017). "Jean Patou." Available at: http://www.thefullwiki.org/Jean_Patou (accessed 4 October 2017).

Thurman, J. (1982). *Isak Dinesen: The Life of Karen Blixen.* London: Weidenfeld and Nicolson.

Twain, M. (1878/2010). *The Adventures of Tom Sawyer.* Melbourne: Penguin Group.

Ziegler, M., and P. Ziegler. (1986). *Banana Republic: Guide to Travel and Safari Clothing.* New York: Ballantine Books.

Figure credits

Figure 1

"View over the Castle Ashby ha-ha," 2005. Image courtesy of Brookie at the Wikimedia Commons. CC BY-SA 3.0. https://creativecommons.org/licenses/by-sa/3.0/

Figure 2

"30 St Mary Axe from Leadenhall Street," 2010. Image courtesy of Aurelian Guichard at the Wikimedia Commons. CC BY-SA 2.0. https://creativecommons.org/licenses/by-sa/2.0/

Figure 3

"9091 (Bollitore) for Alessi," 1983. Image courtesy of Christos Vittoratos at the Wikimedia Commons. CC BY-SA 3.0. https://creativecommons.org/licenses/by-sa/3.0/

Figure 4

"Teatro Olimpico, Bühnenwand," 2005. Image courtesy of Peter Geymayer at Wikimedia Commons. https://commons.wikimedia.org/w/index.

Figure 5

"Couple in love at the 2010 Carnevale in Venice," 2010. Image courtesy of Frank Kovlachek at the English Language Wikipedi. CC BY-SA 2.0. https://creativecommons.org/licenses/by-sa/2.0/

Figure 6

"Minox B (1958)," 2013. Image courtesy of Dnalor 01 at the Wikimedia Commons. CC BY-SA 3.0. https://creativecommons.org/licenses/by-sa/3.0/

Figure 7

"The Offenbach Model," redesigned by the author.

Figure 8

"Porsche Carrera," 2006. Image courtesy of Stahlkocher at the Wikimedia Commons. CC BY-SA 3.0. https://creativecommons.org/licenses/by-sa/3.0/

Figure 9

"Second inauguration of Barack Obama," 2012. Image courtesy of Djembayz at the Wikimedia Commons. CC BY-SA 3.0. https://creativecommons.org/licenses/by-sa/3.0/

Figure 10

"Members of Anonymous Outside the Queen Victoria Street Scientology HQ," 2008. Image courtesy of James Harrison at the Wikimedia Commons.

Figure 11

"Vienna Magic." Image courtesy of the author.

Figure 12

"Chanel Cambon, 31 Rue Cambon, 75001 Paris, Fance," 2011. Image courtesy of Chris Waits at the Wikimedia Commons. CC BY-SA 2.0. https://creativecommons.org/licenses/by-sa/2.0/

Figure 13

Gucci magazine advertisement, 2015. Image courtesy of The Advertising Archives.

Figure 14

Clairol magazine advertisement, 1957. Image courtesy of The Advertising Archives.

Figure 15

Estée Lauder magazine advertisement, 2012. Image courtesy of The Advertising Archives.

Figure 16

Woman with a Parasol, 1875, oil on canvas, Claude Monet.

Figure 17

Neutrogena magazine advertisement, 2000s. Image courtesy of the Advertising Archive.

Figure 18

Casablanca, 1942. Image courtesy of the GAB Archive/Redferns and Getty Images.

Figure 19

"Dinner by Heston Blumenthal—Mandarin Oriental, Hyde Park, London," 2011. Image courtesy of irene at the Wikimedia Commons. CC BY-SA 2.0. https://creativecommons.org/licenses/by-sa/2.0/

Figure 20

"The Sainsbury Wing of the National Gallery, London, UK," 2006. Image courtesy of Richard George at the Wikimedia Commons. CC BY-SA 3.0. https://creativecommons.org/licenses/by-sa/3.0/

Figure 21

"The Museum of Archaeology in Skopje," 2013. Image courtesy of Local hero at the Wikimedia Commons. CC BY-SA 3.0. https://creativecommons.org/licenses/by-sa/3.0/

Figure 22

"The Chiat/Day Building (1991), by Frank Gehry, in Venice, California," 2007. Image courtesy of Bobak Ha'Eri at the Wikimedia Commons. CC BY-SA 3.0. https://creativecommons.org/licenses/by-sa/3.0/

Figure 23

"Bibliothèque nationale de France, one of the four angular-shaped buildings," 2011. Image courtesy of Adriano at the French Language Wikipedia. CC BY-SA 2.5. https://creativecommons.org/licenses/by-sa/2.5/

Figure 24

"The five architectural orders," from Diderot's *Encyclopédie*. Image courtesy of the author.

Figure 25

"Facade of the church Saint-Gervais, Saint-Protais in Paris," 2010. Image

courtesy of Tangopaso at the Wikimedia Commons. https://commons.wikimedia.
org/w/index.php?search=Facade+of+the+church+Saint-Gervais%2C+Saint-Prota
is+in+Paris&title=Special:Search&go=Go&searchToken=4lh3ps7v9jshhsae8rr22
b9cf#/media/File:Facade_St-Gervais_St-Protais.jpg

Figure 26

"Amalienborg med C.F. Harsdorffs kolonnade," 2010. Image courtesy of
Trond Arild Ydersbond at the Wikimedia Commons. CC BY-SA 4.0. https://
creativecommons.org/licenses/by-sa/4.0/

Figure 27

"Doric columns, Athena temple, Paestum, Italy," 2008. Image courtesy of
Heinz-Josef Lücking at the Wikimedia Commons. CC BY-SA 3.0. https://
creativecommons.org/licenses/by-sa/3.0/

Figure 28

"Potemkin stairs," 2005. Image courtesy of Dezidor at Wikimedia Commons.

Figure 29

"Trier—Basilica of Constantine (Aula Palatina)," 2013. Image courtesy of Pudelek
at the Wikimedia Commons. CC BY-SA 3.0. https://creativecommons.org/
licenses/by-sa/3.0/

Figure 30

"Konstantinbasilik in Trier," 2008. Image courtesy of Berthold Werner at the
Wikimedia Commons.

Figure 31

"The University of Melbourne." Image courtesy of the author.

Figure 32

"Base of the Hearst Tower, New York, NY," 2008. Image courtesy of
Alex Maisuradze at the Wikimedia Commons. CC BY-SA 4.0. https://
creativecommons.org/licenses/by-sa/4.0/

Figure 33

"Castle Ashby ha-ha with the Orangery in the background," 2005. Image
courtesy Brookie at the Wikimedia Commons. CC BY-SA 3.0. https://
creativecommons.org/licenses/by-sa/3.0/

Figure 34

"The ha-ha principle." Image courtesy of the author.

Figure 35

"'Wassily' Club Chair (Mode B3)," late 1927 or early 1928, Marcel Breuer. Image
courtesy of the Museum of Modern Art, New York/Scala, Florence.

Figure 36

"Easy chair," 1928, Le Corbusier, Pierre Jeanneret, and Charlotte Perriand.
Manufacturer: Heidi Weber. Gift of Phyllis B. Lambert. Acc. Num. 337.1960.a-f ©
2018. Courtesy of the Museum of Modern Art, New York/Scala, Florence.

Figure 37

"Villa Savoye, exterior." Image courtesy of Ben Olson.

Figure 38

"Villa Savoye, exterior with 'maritime' details." Image courtesy of Ben Olson.

Figure 39

Escaping Criticism, 1874, oil on canvas, Pere Borrell del Caso.

Figure 40

"Scuola Grande di San Marco, devant San Zanipolo, à Venise," 2012. Image Courtesy of Remi Mathis at the Wikimedia Commons. CC BY-SA 3.0. https://creativecommons.org/licenses/by-sa/3.0/

Figure 41

"Jesuit Church, Vienna, Austria," 2006. Image courtesy of Albert Fernandez Fernandez at the Wikimedia Commons. CC BY-SA 3.0. https://creativecommons.org/licenses/by-sa/3.0/

Figure 42

"Grand Canal Shoppes." Image courtesy of the author.

Figure 43

"Replica of the Austrian town Hallstatt in China," 2013. Image courtesy of Hanno Böck at the Wikimedia Commons. CC BY-SA 4.0. https://creativecommons.org/licenses/by-sa/4.0/

Figure 44

"The Imitation of a British Town …," 2006. Image courtesy of Huai-Chun Hsu at Flckr. CC BY-SA 2.0. https://creativecommons.org/licenses/by/2.0/

Figure 45

"Thames Town," 2012. Image courtesy of Maurice Latzke at the English Language Wikipedia. CC BY-SA 3.0. https://creativecommons.org/licenses/by-sa/3.0/

Figure 46

"Reproduced Gustavian Chair, Medevi Brunn," 1997, Move Møbler. Image courtesy of the Nationalmuseum Stockholm.

Figure 47

"Cartier Santo-Dumont, 1910." M. Gérard, Cartier Collection © Cartier.

Figure 48

"The Big Pilot's Watch." Image courtesy of IWC Schaffhausen.

Figure 49

"Rolex Oyster Perpetual Sea-Dweller," 2009. Image Courtesy of Rruegger at the Wikimedia Commons. CC BY-SA 3.0. https://creativecommons.org/licenses/by-sa/3.0/

Figure 50

"Boat shoes," Bastian Andersen. Image courtesy of the photographer.

Figure 51

"Massive Winter Storm Brings Snow and Heavy Winds Across Large Swath of Eastern Seaboard," Mark Wilson. Image courtesy of Getty Images.

Figure 52

"Amateur Me Bicyclists competing in the Garrett Lemire Memorial Grand Prix National Racing Circuit (NRC) on April 10, 2005 in Ojai, CA," Joe Sohm/Visions of America. Image courtesy of Getty Images.

Figure 53

"March 6, 1912: Titanic (right) had to be moved out of the drydock so her sister Olympic (left), which had lost a propeller, could have it replaced," 1912, Robert John Welch (1859–1936). Image courtesy of Masur at the Wikimedia Commons.

Figure 54

"Mac trash can icon." Screenshot by author.

Figures 55, 56, and 57

"iPhone with Skeuomorph icons." Screenshots by author.

Figure 58

"The Burberry Trench-Warm," 1916. Image courtesy of the author.

Figure 59

"Reigate Heath," 2009. Image Courtesy of Allen Watkin at the Wikimedia Commons. CC BY-SA 2.0. https://creativecommons.org/licenses/by-sa/2.0/

Figure 60

"1986 Chrysler LeBaron Town & Country Station Wagon—with the fake wood paneling and alloy wheels," 2009. Image courtesy of dave_7 at Flickr. CC BY-SA 2.0. https://creativecommons.org/licenses/by-sa/2.0/

Figure 61

"Fullbrogue (Grenson)," 2005. Image courtesy of Rainer Ersfeld at the Wikimedia Commons. CC BY-SA 2.5. https://creativecommons.org/licenses/by-sa/2.5/

Figure 62

"Original factory wire wheel cover on a 1967 AMC Marlin (American Motors Corporation) with vintage US Royal 'Tiger Paw' red-stripe high-performance 8.25 x 14 nylon bias belt tires," 2005. Image courtesy of Christopher Ziemnowicz at the Wikimedia Commons. CC BY-SA 2.5. https://creativecommons.org/licenses/by-sa/2.5/

Figure 63

"The Venetian, Macao." Image courtesy of the author.

Figure 64

"Arts et Metiers metro station in Paris," 2010. Image courtesy of Stephen Butterworth at the Wikimedia Commons. CC BY-SA 2.0. https://creativecommons.org/licenses/by-sa/2.0/

Figure 65

"Picture of the Telectroscope art installation aperture at City Hall in London," 2008. Image courtesy of Colonel Warde at the Wikimedia Commons. CC BY-SA 3.0. https://creativecommons.org/licenses/by-sa/3.0/

Figure 66

"Street Style—New York City—February 2017," Michael Stewart. Image courtesy of Getty Images.

Figure 67

"Grapes," Stig Nørhald. Image courtesy of the artist.

Figure 68

"Banana," Stig Nørhald. Image courtesy of the artist.

Figure 69'

"Lime," Stig Nørhald. Image courtesy of the artist.

Figure 70

"Elk head trophy in the Château de Tanlay, Yonne Department, Burgundy, France," 2014. Image courtesy of Myrabella at the Wikimedia Commons. CC BY-SA 4.0. https://creativecommons.org/licenses/by-sa/4.0/

Figure 71

"Otto Klepper, Prussian Minister of Finance," 1931. Image courtesy of Getty Images.

Figure 72

Banana Republic advertisement.

Figure 73

Ralph Lauren magazine ad.

Figure 74

"Aquadome, Lalandia i Billund," 2010. Image courtesy of lalanida.dk at the Danish Language Wikipedia. CC BY-SA 2.5. https://creativecommons.org/licenses/by-sa/2.5/

Figure 75

"Formica," Stig Nørhald. Image courtesy of the artist.

Figure 76

"Fake carbon fiber." Screen shot by author.

Figure 77

"Fake checker plate." Screen shot by author.

Figure 78

"PARO mental commitment robot," 1993, designed by Takanori Shibata. Image courtesy of AIST, Japan.

Figure 79

"Pleo robot," 2009. Image courtesy of Jiuguang Wang at the Wikimedia Commons. CC SA-BY 3.0. https://creativecommons.org/licenses/by/3.0/

Figure 80

"Gliedermann," 2018, René Birkholm. Image courtesy of René Birkholm, tegneren.dk.

Figure 81

"Plastic food samples displayed in a restaurant window," 2007. Image courtesy of Lombroso at the Wikimedia Commons, https://commons.wikimedia.org/w/index.php?title=Special:Search&title=Special:Search&redirs=0&search=Plastic+food+samples+displayed+in+a+restaurant+window&fulltext=Search&fulltext=Advanced+search&ns0=1&ns6=1&ns14=1&advanced=1&searchToken=7kr-

flv56emryq0pkzzj9eauxd#/media/File:Food_samples_1.jpg.

Figure 82

"Set 21007 is modeled after New York City's Rockefeller Center. It consists of 240 pieces and is rated Age 10+," 2012. Image courtesy of InSapphoWeTrust at the Wikimedia Commons. CC SA-BY 2.0. https://creativecommons.org/licenses/by/2.0/

Figure 83

"Doctor's Lady," Horst Kuh. Image courtesy of the artist.

Figure 84

"Roo," Lynette Zeeng. Image courtesy of the artist.

Figure 85

"Scarecrow," Stig Nørhald. Image courtesy of the artist.

Figure 86

"Vendetta masks marketed by Amazon." Screen shot by author.

Figure 87

"Stamp Antarctica," Stig Nørhald. Image courtesy of the artist.

Figure 88

"Stamp Falkland," Stig Nørhald. Image courtesy of the artist.

Figure 89

Theatrum Orbis Terrarum, 1574, Abraham Ortelius. Image courtesy of the author.

Figure 90

"London A-Z Ski Slope Haggerston." Image courtesy of the author.

Figure 91

"Illustration from Histoire des Jouets," 2014. Image courtesy of the Internet Archive at the Wikimedia Commons.

Figure 92

"Theresienstadt concentration camp archway," 2013. Image courtesy of Andrew Shiva at the Wikimedia Commons. CC BY-SA 4.0. https://creativecommons.org/licenses/by/4.0/

Figure 93

"A view of the North Korean village Kijong-dong, also known as 'propaganda village,'" 1987. Image courtesy of Don Sutherland at the Wikimedia Commons.

Figure 94

"Acanthoxyla prasina or prickly stick insect, found in Fairfield, Otago, New Zealand," 2012. Image courtesy of Alan Gilchrist at the Wikimedia Commons. CC BY-SA 3.0. https://creativecommons.org/licenses/by/3.0/

Figure 95

"Male specimen—Ventral side," 2011. Image courtesy of Didier Descouens at the Wikimedia Commons. CC By-SA 3.0. https://creativecommons.org/licenses/by/3.0/

Figure 96

"A young red-necked wallaby Macropus rufogriseus taken in Ensay, Victoria,

Australia," 2007. Image courtesy of benjamint444 at the Wikimedia Commons. CC SA-BY 3.0. https://creativecommons.org/licenses/by/3.0/

Figure 97

"Methar [sic] Lam, Afghanistan," 2005. Image courtesy of Cpl. James L. Yarboro, U.S. Marine Corps, at the English Language Wikipedia.

Figure 98

"US Army testing the Future Force Warrior components," 2007. Image courtesy of Silent Sentry at the Wikimedia Commons.

Figure 99

"Olympic with Returned Soldiers," 1919, oil on canvas, Arthur Lismer. Image courtesy of the Wikimedia Commons.

Figure 100

"A US Air Forces (USAF) F-117A Nighthawk Stealth Fighter," 2002. Image courtesy of Staff Sgt. Aaron Allmon II at the Wikimedia Commons.

Figure 101

"Swedish corvette HMS Visby in the harbor of Visby," 2006. Image courtesy of Mr Bullitt at the Wikimedia Commons.

Figure 102

"Heddon lure," Stig Nørhald. Image courtesy of the artist.

Figure 103

"Decoys," Stig Nørhald. Image courtesy of the artist.

Figure 104

"Scarecrow," Stig Nørhald. Image courtesy of the artist.

Index